THE ESSENCE OF UNDERSTANDING!

There are no rules or restrictions on what you create. In this private realm *you* are god and you can create exactly what you want! No one else can guide you because your Shangri-la *must* be entirely your own creation. See it— *create* it—in as complete detail as you can, because you will come to it often; the more detailed, complete, and comfortable you can make it now, the more real and inviting to your mind it will be when you seek to return. And you will take refuge here frequently enough for it to become a familiar home.

DEATH BRINGS MANY SURPRISES

Robert H. Coddington

IVY BOOKS • NEW YORK

Ivy Books
Published by Ballantine Books
Copyright © 1987 by Robert H. Coddington

Library of Congress Catalog Card Number: 87-90786

ISBN 0-8041-0128-0

Manufactured in the United States of America

First Edition: July 1987

Table of Contents

Preface

If this were played upon a stage now, I could condemn it as improbable fiction.

—Shakespeare
Twelfth Night

Do not believe this book.

Don't take what it says at face value; take it as a challenge. As a challenge to limited concepts of reality, as a kaleidoscopic telescope to extend your vision of possibilities, as a catalyst for greatly enlarging your self-awareness, identity, and purpose. If you're a curious newcomer to the universe of metaphysics—which is what this book is about—you'll find a conceptual foundation from which you can proceed to explore and construct your own unique belief structure.

Belief is placement of faith in an unknown, a risk that some are unwilling to take. Yet if it is true, as these pages allege, that one's personal "reality" is only a belief structure that works, the distinction between *known* and *unknown* becomes indeterminate and the risk of believing turns out to be one only of degree. So here you will find

ix

some interrelated concepts to reflect upon and weigh against your own standards of logic and belief. If your belief structure is not one of closed, stagnant dogma, if you are stimulated by concepts that sometimes force you to reexamine your old beliefs and explore new ones, try these. Evaluate each concept for its "feel" of rightness, its acceptability to you—above all, its *workability*—were you to integrate it into your belief structure. Then accept it, or reject it, or hold it in limbo as you choose.

By the time this book sees print, even *I* won't believe parts of it. Having an elastic belief structure, I can—and do—tentatively accept, revise, and discard concepts as my growing knowledge and experience may dictate. What I'm doing here is urging you throughout to do the same: to avoid uncritical acceptance of *any* other's claims to truth; to open your possibility thinking and to evaluate all concepts according to your judgment and the guidance of your own higher consciousness before you accept them into your body of personal belief.

Exploration, self-reliance, and self-determination are the underlying credo of these pages. This book discusses your relationship to unseen worlds but, since absolute truth is so evanescent, it presents only suggested truths of those worlds. These are concepts of metaphysical "realities" that some persons have found to work and therefore have accepted as personal beliefs to nurture and to live by until better ones come to light. Make of these concepts what you will—but should you play the intractably negative skeptic all your life only to find that death brings many surprises, don't come back to haunt me with the complaint that you weren't warned!

Chapter 1

A PIECE OF MY MIND

The mind of each man is the man himself.
— Marcus Tullius Cicero
De Oratore I

"Patrick, won't you say hello to us?"

I knew the question was addressed to me, but my name is Robert. Or Bob. Certainly not Patrick. And Bruce Born *knew* that. Sitting in a chair facing the audience, my eyes closed, I supposedly had been placed in a light trance, but I felt fully aware and I certainly knew my name was Robert. Not even my middle name is Patrick; yet I felt a strange urge to respond.

Bruce Born is a researcher and teacher who, with his psychic wife, Jeann, was introducing me to a course in metaphysics[1]. And he very well knew my

---

[1] A philosophical structure of transcendental or supersensible realities.

given name. I felt that answering to any other name while I ostensibly was in a trance but in fact felt fully aware would mislead the rapt audience and contribute to a deception.

But the urge to answer to "Patrick" became stronger, and I grew troubled; whence came this urge to conspire in Born's flamboyant attempt to confirm a basic tenet of his teaching? I certainly didn't want to give it false validity through any form of deceit, however unintentional. Then, in the midst of this struggle with my conscience, I felt my lips twitch involuntarily, my teeth part, and I heard my voice say, "Hello."

So much for good intentions! On the conscious level, anyway. Evidently there was some other aspect of me that had a mind of its own, so to speak. And speak it did, even as I consciously resisted cooperating with it.

According to Born and some other metaphysics researchers, each of us has another level of consciousness, the *Superconscious*, which is capable of independent thought, knowledge, and actions[2]. This exercise was an experiment in which my ordinary consciousness ostensibly was led into a passive state so that this higher consciousness could by-pass it and speak directly through my vocal cords. It seemed to work.

Perhaps I should, in referring to this higher consciousness, say *who* is capable of independent thought, etc., since events do seem to bear out the

---

[2]The concept of the Superconscious was promulgated earlier in this century by the late Edgar Cayce, the Seer of Virginia Beach, and is inherent in the belief structures of a number of schools of metaphysics.

contention that your higher self has a personality distinct from the conscious you; one that—even though it is an aspect of the *total* you—merits a name of its own. Ergo "Patrick," a name that had some significance to me at that moment.

Bruce and Jeann Born were instrumental in indoctrinating hundreds of seekers with this concept of a distinct higher personality. Their Jupiter Movement—an educational enterprise so named for Jupiter's symbolic representation of Heaven in Born's cosmology—was established in several eastern and southern U.S. cities in the seventies and eighties, touching the lives of many. It teaches the acceptance as practical reality of the existence of each individual's superconscious higher mind and personality. And the premise of the superconscious mind is the fundamental tenet underlying all concepts in this book.

The very act of slicing from your totality an aspect so distinct, so independently volitional as to merit its own name, takes a certain courage. This higher self is *not* the alter ego of Jekyll's Hyde, or a personality dissociation as manifested in the multiple faces of Eve, or a threat to your sanity. For most of us, it is a potential ally in our selection of life's pathways, but it is our ordinary *conscious* mind that remains the instrument of our free will and is the instigator of most of our actions—and which sometimes thwarts the good intentions of our Superconscious.

To contemplate the existence of the Superconscious is to infer that there is some "higher" aspect of the individual that has thus far remained

3

obscure to orthodox science, including that body of opinionated structures we call psychology. The independent *sentience* displayed by the Superconscious sets it apart from the stimulus-response nature of the subconscious; neither does it conform to Skinnerian behaviorism nor to Freudian id/ego concepts. It is not a manifestation of instinct; it is a *thinking* mentality with memories, opinions, motivations, and access to knowledge beyond that normally available to the individual's conventional consciousness. And, while science admits of no physiological vehicle to accommodate higher levels of mentality, traditional religious concepts allow one: *the Superconscious is the mind of the Spirit.*

Heavens! Merely *mentioning* spiritual realms is a turn-off to some readers, isn't it? Those who can't even speculate about realms of nonphysical existence—those who have an irrational fear of unproven concepts—may as well give up right here, because most of this book deals with the superconscious mind of the Spirit and alternate realities. Not with religion; not with main line religious dogmas; but with spiritual realities as they are said to exist by entities active in spiritual realms.

Because it appears that existence and identity at superconscious levels must transcend our commonly perceived physical reality, even a tentative acceptance of this concept invites consideration and attempted verification of alternate reality structures and their implications for our "real" world. We'll digress briefly from the role of the superconscious mind to explore reality in the next chapter, where you will see that what you commonly think of as "reality" is highly illusory, at best.

Before I try to stretch your personal reality structure, discussion of a few of the specialized terms frequently used in this book is in order. A couple of them—like *superconscious*—already have sneaked in, and it's important to define their meanings as used here, because many are rather broadly and variously used in the literature of metaphysics.

And there's a good place to start: *metaphysics*. Literally, this should refer to a physical science transcending that of *physics*, but scientists have not succeeded (nor tried in any concerted manner) to ascertain the fundamental rules that would define metaphysics as a science. It therefore usually is defined as a *philosophy* of transcendental realities, or a philosophy that investigates first principles and the nature of reality. In a sense, this is convenient; this book is about metaphysics and, since metaphysics is a philosophy rather than a science, its validity does not rest on scientific proof.

A student or practitioner of metaphysics traditionally is called a *metaphysician*. I think this may be appropriate for one who has the gift of channeling healing energy into a subject's body, but is not so for others. A student or researcher of physics is a physicist; I believe a student or researcher of metaphysics should be termed a *metaphysicist*.

Sometimes the word metaphysics is used to denote the so-called *supernatural*. In the sense that the word supernatural pertains to existence beyond the perceived physical world, this is acceptable. However, supernatural also may connote the *miraculous*, which is not in accord with the sense of metaphysics as the word is used in this book. Much of what is purported to be supernatural can be viewed as entirely natural when seen from the metaphysical point of view.

Discarnate is an adjective meaning "without a physical body." Used to describe a Spirit or soul in the classical sense, without a physical, mortal body. Also, *disincarnate*.

Incarnate, used as an adjective, means "enclosed by (or possessing) a physical, mortal body." As a verb, it means to be born on the physical plane with a mortal body.

A *medium* is a person through whom nonphysical aspects of other individuals (who may be either physically living or existing only in the discarnate state) may manifest, usually through communication via the medium's vocal chords, but also via automatic writing or other manipulation of the medium's body.

Occult is a word with strong emotional overtones for many. Its literal meaning is simply *hidden*, which is innocuous enough, but to many, it carries a connotation of dark or evil forces at work casting spells, invoking negative forces, etc. Because of this narrow and charged meaning, I prefer not to use the word; if I do so, it is used only in a neutral sense to distinguish its object from ordinary reality.

Paranormal literally means "almost normal," a roundabout way of saying "not normal." It is another of those words used to signify things and events that can't be explained by our conventional concepts of reality; a synonym for "supernatural" that doesn't imply the miraculous.

Parapsychology is to psychology what metaphysics is to physics: an attempt to dignify a study of the paranormal with a name resembling an academic discipline. Metaphysics may profess to deal more with the impersonal structures and cause-and-effect relationships of alternate realities; parapsychology may concentrate on the psychic aspects of telepathy, clairvoyance, etc. Yet the phenomena of interest seem to be so closely interwoven as to make the words metaphysics and parapsychology virtually synonymous, and they are used interchangeably here.

Psychic is an adjective much used here and elsewhere, pertaining to so-called extrasensory mental

7

capabilities, such as telepathy, clairvoyance, and numerous others. Used as a noun, it refers to a person allegedly gifted with one or more psychic abilities. It is used here much in these same senses but is attributed to powers of the Superconscious, as will become evident.

Soul is one of those words that means widely varying things to different persons. Although it is often used interchangeably with *Spirit*, there seems to be an additional, distinct aspect of the total man that could be termed the soul, so I prefer to separate the words and simply avoid soul except as it may be tentatively suggested and narrowly qualified in the text where it is used.

Spirit is a biggie in this book. As used here, Spirit means a noncorporeal, individual *persona*, embodying the holographic element of omniscience and the spark of divinity that it inherited in its separation from the Godhead eons ago. In following the command to experience the universe and return, Spirits enter into mortal human form for the physical cycle, but endure in nonphysical realms beyond mortal death.

The *trance* state is erroneously believed by many to mean that a person is in a state of suspended awareness; that the conscious mind in trance always is blanked out, thereby giving a hypnotist access to the subconscious or opening a channel for communication with higher sources. It is true that one's conscious awareness may be turned off during a *deep* trance, but *any* waking state in which the predominant brain-wave activity shifts to a slower rate (as can be observed by an encephalograph)[3] is entrancing. There is a continuous spectrum of trance states, from the very lightest to those so deep that bodily functions appear to cease. Persons in *light* trance retain full awareness and usually doubt that they are in fact in an altered state; yet light trance (alternatively called the *alpha state*) is the most common state of receptivity used for meditation, both externally directed and self-induced hypnosis, mediumship, and various other psychic manifestations. Each of us spends more waking time in some level of trance than we imagine.

Transcendent literally means "rising or existing above." Transcendent reality may or may not exist "above" ordinary reality in a literal sense, but it is widely believed to do so in the figurative sense of being exalted above all the petty imperfections and flaws of physical existence.

---

[3]Electrical waves generated by the brain during fully attentive mental activity are termed *beta* waves, which have a repetition rate on the order of sixteen to twenty per second. The first level of trance brings *alpha* waves, about ten to twelve per second, into dominance. Deeper trance states move into the *delta*-wave region. Below this lies the *theta*-wave region, which accompanies a state of suspended animation that appears to resemble death.

It is inevitable that some of these near synonyms are used interchangeably in these pages devoted to the paranormal. Or should I say, the psychic? Or metaphysical? Maybe far out? I trust you won't find them confusing.

Numerous other words used in this book have various shades of meaning in a metaphysical context. They will be defined as they are introduced.

Now, on to reality. . . .

Chapter 2

REALITY ISN'T REAL

Appearances to the mind are of four kinds. Things either are what they appear to be; or they neither are, nor appear to be; or they are, and do not appear to be; or they are not, and yet appear to be. Rightly to aim in all these cases is the wise man's task.

—Epictetus
Discourses, Chapter 27

If I am to stimulate your curiosity about the metaphysical universe, I must first manage somehow to stretch your view of possible reality beyond that of those who are merely rational. This is the objective of this chapter.

My well-thumbed and venerable copy of *Webster*'s says, "*Real* implies agreement between what a thing seems to be and what it is."[1] This seemingly reasonable definition assumes that reality is a fixed, absolute structure external to and independ-

---

[1] *Webster's Seventh New Collegiate Dictionary.* Springfield, MA: G. & C. Merriam, 1963.

ent of human perception or thought. This reality structure presumably encompasses all physical objects, natural laws, and known entities having a state of existence—an "is-ness." But what we unthinkingly accept as day-to-day reality fails this presumption. It fails because we cannot truly define what *is*.

To examine this problem of definition, let's start with something close at hand. In fact, with this book *in* your hand. You'll surely agree that it's real. Most people would describe it as a physical object having a mass of several ounces (which can be measured), with breadth, length, and thickness (also measurable). It is equipped with front and back covers, enclosing a considerable number of paper pages covered with printing. Very mundane; *everybody* knows how a book is structured. In other words, it has *objective reality*, which simply means that everyone who examines it will agree on its essential details. However, that "objective reality" is only an illusion!

Scientists tell us that this book really is comprised mostly of *nothing*. Scattered within the volume of space it occupies are molecules of matter arranged in various combinations to produce the different characteristics of paper, ink, glue, etc., and arrayed to form page surfaces and edges, binding, typeface images, and all the other apparent physical and chemical properties of a book.

Moreover, those widely scattered molecules are further divisible into atoms. Each atom, in turn, contains a nucleus about which individual electrons orbit at inconceivable velocities. The distances

12

separating the nucleus and its orbiting atoms are comparable, on a microcosmic scale, to those between the sun and its orbiting planets, meaning that even the atoms are made mostly of empty space!

So this book is "really" just a very large number of atoms, with their spinning nuclei and their orbiting electrons enclosing mostly nothing, arranged in latticelike patterns to form molecules as are your body, your house, the oceans, mountains, etc. The molecules also contain much empty space and, at any temperature above absolute zero, are themselves in motion and separated from one another. This doesn't sound much like the inert, solid package of bound pages you thought you were holding, does it? Yet the physicist insists that this is much closer to the book's absolute reality than is the illusion you perceive. And he and his colleagues are busily trying to peel still more layers of illusion away from the nature of matter, probing ever more deeply into the structures of the subnuclear particles of matter. It may turn out that there is no such thing as physical matter at all; Einstein derived a mathematical expression about sixty years ago which suggests that matter is nothing more than incredibly concentrated packets of energy.

So how does all of this relate to your perception of this book? I bring it up only to illustrate how something you've taken all your life to be real actually is an illusion caused by the limitations of your senses. This is no fault of yours; if your eyes could resolve details as small as those revealed by the electron microscope, you could perceive in this book some of the structures deduced by the physicists. Lacking this, the physical reality you perceive here is only a convenient—and mutually accepted—illusion.

There is nothing wrong with an inexact or illusory reality structure; any society must have a "practical reality" upon which it can agree. If it *works* for that society, then we can't say it's wrong. *But it is erroneous to think of this "reality" as external, absolute, and unchangeable.* To do so is to obscure the truth that reality lies in the mind of the beholder; that *your* only reality resides within you; and that you have the power to expand and restructure that reality as your own knowledge and experience dictate. *It is essential for you to understand that your reality is not bound by the limitations that society at large endeavors to impose on it.*

That's the crucial point: From the standpoint of practical application it's not important that a perception is an illusion, if it *works*. It applies as well to this book: Even though what you seem to see differs greatly from its underlying physical reality, this book serves its intended purpose of recording, storing, and disseminating communication from one individual to many others, and for this use, it doesn't matter the least bit if its apparent reality is an illusion. It is what I choose to call an *objective practical reality*. Practical because it works, and objective because most observers agree on the essentials of its apparent reality and usefulness. And there's nothing unique about this book; practically all of physical reality is equally illusory at the level of direct human perception.

14

Having thus undermined your understanding of "reality" by showing that what we commonly perceive and accept as reality is in fact largely structured illusion, I now must go a step further: you *cannot experience* objective reality. By definition, what you experience can only be *subjective*. While you may agree with others about the shape, weight, colors, and other perceptions of this book and thereby reach a consensus as to its objective practical reality, the fact remains that your personal perception of it can *only* be subjective. It is your mind's interpretation of the various stimuli it receives from your sensory organs that creates your image of this book's physical characteristics—an entirely subjective image. We know from the foregoing that this image is an illusion; yet *it works*.

How does it feel to realize that you're reading nothing more than a subjective illusion? Does your knowledge that its absolute physical reality—if in fact there *is* such a thing—is vastly unlike this illusion detract one whit from its function as a medium of communication? Of course not. This book is what I call a *subjective practical reality*.

But of course *all* your reality is subjective. And most of it is illusory. So how can you separate reality from delusion? The key word to your personal reality is in the phrase above: *practical*. The test of personal reality is simply to ask yourself this: does it work for *me*? If so, then it's a subjective practical reality. If it doesn't, then it's not "real."

The key to subjective reality lies in the word *believe*. Reality is a matter of *belief*, not of absolute fact. This frees you to define your own reality concepts—which form your *beliefs*—without concerning yourself over their acceptance by others. It's *your* reality; structure it as you like. *Provided* . . .

Provided that you faithfully adhere to this fundamental requirement: your belief must work for you! If, for instance, you choose to believe that you are a reincarnation of Napoleon, then patterning your personality, your drive, and your determination after his may be very effective for reaching your goals. This belief could work positively for you, if this is what it takes to inspire those characteristics in yourself. However, if you profess in the presence of skeptics to *be* Napoleon reincarnated and expect them to share your belief and defer to your wishes, desires, and intents because of whom you believe you are, you may be assured that it *won't* work—unless your goal is to partake of institutional life for the rest of your days. Personal realities at odds with the accepted norm can work only so long as they don't incur inimical responses from others. It's okay for you to believe you're Napoleon; it's not okay to ask others to believe you are. Society deems those who can't distinguish fantasy from "objective" reality to be insane, and *that* label works for practically no one.

Now that you see that reality is only subjective for each of us, and that no one can say with certainty what is the absolute nature underlying those illusions we call physical reality, you are free to adjust some of your lifelong thinking habits. Give yourself permission, right now, to entertain conditional belief in something—*anything*—that you never before accepted. Conditional belief, because you can't justify unconditional belief until you try the subject to see if it works for you. If it does, you can cement your belief; if it doesn't, you can discard it even though it may seem to work for others.

Before you're overcome by the headiness of your new freedom to believe, let's look for a moment at the other side of the coin: can you be equally as subjective about *dis*belief? Can you reject with impunity any beliefs that are widely held by most of society? The answer is *no*. The fact that a physical object isn't really constructed as we perceive it to be does not mean that there's not *something* there; something that can impose destructive and even fatal rearrangement of the illusion that you call your physical body! Disbelief in the *underlying* reality of something physical, however it may differ from its apparent reality, won't *work* for you and therefore is not a valid disbelief.

A valid *dis*belief? Yes, for what is a disbelief but an inverted belief? To belabor the example, disbelief in the material reality of an automobile is belief in its nonmateriality, which would be a downright hazardous belief—a belief that won't work. And this workability criterion for belief/nonbelief extends to immaterial structures as well. You may disbelieve that society has the right to impose its laws on you, but act on that premise and sooner or later you'll find it doesn't work for you. The measure of any belief or disbelief—of any per-

17

sonal reality structure—is, *how does it work* for you?

On the positive side, though, those concepts do give you new freedom to disbelieve a philosophical tenet in the face of its overwhelming acceptance by others. The old saying that "Fifty-million Frenchmen can't be wrong" *is* wrong. Of course fifty million—or five-hundred million—can be wrong, and *you* can be right. How many people once believed the world was flat? How many scientists today believe that material velocities beyond the speed of light are impossible, or more than once believed nothing could fly through the air faster than the speed of sound? How many people today automatically limit their achievement potential by their disbeliefs in possibilities, which is to say, beliefs in impossibilities? No one ever breached an obstacle that he believed was absolutely impossible to breach. So the freedom to question the validity of commonly perceived "realities"; the realization that you don't have to blindly accept society's "truths" without testing their workability in your own reality structure, is a bonus benefit of this new permission you have given yourself to believe— and by extension, to disbelieve—as you deem fit.

Let's see how this freedom to disbelieve one of society's "truths" might work in practice. Take the emotion of anger, for instance. Volumes have been written by psychologists and others about coping with anger, all implicitly assuming that anger is an inevitable response to certain external circumstances inflicted on the individual. This is *not* a truth (real); it's a *belief*. If you view external circumstances or individuals as causes of your anger, you're nurturing a belief. Built upon this belief, you perceive the following realities:

1. You sometimes experience anger. This is a subjective reality, certainly.
2. You blame your anger on circumstances or individuals external to yourself. Fallacious in fact, but real enough within the framework of your belief.
3. You allow others to control you ("He makes me so mad!").
4. You feel no direct responsibility for your anger.

This belief will "work" for you, bringing to your subjective reality the known negative physical effects of suppressed anger,the undesirable consequences of angry outbursts made in socially unacceptable ways, the disfavor of those you offend, and the unwitting relinquishment of control of your emotions to other people and even inanimate objects.

But some beliefs—some subjective realities— work better than others. Suppose you believed that *your own thoughts* are the real source of your anger? Suppose you believed that anger, being an emotion, is triggered by your *subjective reaction* to external circumstances, *not* by the circumstances themselves? After all, you can't get angry—regardless of the stimulus—when you're unconscious, can you? Wouldn't this belief lead a rational, thinking person like you to realize that becoming angry is strictly your own choice and is not an inevitable result of external circumstances beyond your control? That you don't *have* to cope with anger, because you can simply elect not to become angry at all?

If you were to embrace this alternate belief, you would create a new subjective reality to supplant the old. Among the ways this new reality could work for you are:

1. You would accept responsibility for your feelings, understanding that you can control them in a responsible manner.
2. You would no longer permit other persons and external events to control your emotions.
3. You would *avoid* anger reactions in circumstances where their display is inappropriate, rather than having to suppress rage to the detriment of your health.
4. In those circumstances where a degree of righteous indignation may spur you to constructive corrective actions, you would generate only an appropriate level of anger, recognizing meanwhile that it is your choice and your conscious decision to allow that anger.

Of these two anger-related beliefs (subjective realities), I find the second one works better for me and those with whom I interact, and I therefore have adopted that reality accordingly. I don't know that my choice is closer to some absolute reality than is the more widely held belief; I only know that it is true for me and will be my reality until I find one that is superior. I certainly feel no compulsion to conform to the psychologists' reality belief when mine works better for me. This is a sample of the way in which exercising the freedom to disbelieve can be beneficial.

Once you understand that absolute, objective reality is unknowable and indefinable, and that practical reality is only a framework of subjective illusions that work, you are freed from all those limitations that heretofore have been imposed on your personal reality structure by a society that has largely come to believe only in what can be detected or deduced by the physical senses.

Now that we've theorized at length about this concept of the subjective nature of reality, would you like to perform an experiment in nonmaterial reality? Would you like to create your own private retreat—your idyllic Shangri-la? You can do so. You can create a structure, right there in your mind, that will be as subjectively real as your powers of imagination can make it. It will have no reality to anyone else, but it can be a remarkably effective hideaway for you—which is to say, it will *work* for you. And that, according to the definitions developed here, makes it a valid personal reality.

It happens that the state of mind most conducive to creativity is the same altered state of consciousness that is sought in meditation exercises. Chapter 14 of this book contains a generalized countdown exercise for entering an open-ended alpha state; if you don't already have your own effective relaxation/meditation exercise, I suggest you refer to the one in Chapter 14 and practice it a few times; or better, have a friend read it aloud while you follow its suggestions.

The object is to reach that inner mental level wherein the mind is relaxed and disengaged from (not necessarily unaware of, but simply unresponsive to) external reality and therefore able to concentrate on imagery you create. Whether by your own exercise or the Chapter 14 countdown, when you have reached that state of consciousness, here are some suggestions to follow:

When you are ready, turn your mind's eye—the one *inside your head*—to your mental-image screen; the same screen you use for sleep dreams, daydreams, and imagination. If it's not blank, wipe it clear and concentrate on the center of it.

Look steadily and intently. Ignore outside sounds, bodily sensations, or stray thoughts. Concentrate on your mental screen. Now, in the very center of that screen, see a tiny pinpoint of intense light. It may be white, or blue, or whatever you personally prefer, but see that it's bright, and it seems to be slowly growing larger!

While you're staring at this expanding point of light, imagine that it's an image that the movie camera of your mind can zoom into and enlarge to fill the screen. In fact, what you are seeing is a very distant view of your own private Shangri-la; your idyllic retreat from the pressures and cares of the external world; and when it zooms in close enough for you to see details, you will find it to be exactly as you desire. But before you zoom in, take just a moment to put your creative powers into perspective.

It is essential for you to understand that there are no rules or restrictions on what you create. In this private realm *you* are god and you can create exactly what you want! Do you prefer a rustic cabin on a windy hill? An opulent mansion on a rolling, green estate? A secure cave in the bowels of a mountain? Or the boughs of a giant tree in a forest where the weather is always perfect? Do you want it here, or on some esoteric planet of your own creation? And how will you furnish it—bare and lean for basic survival, or crowded with material luxuries? Will it be absolutely private, or will you share it with mental images of your friends? No one else can guide you at this point, because your Shangri-la *must* be entirely your own creation. See it—*create* it—in as complete detail as you can, because you will come to it often and the more detailed, complete, and comfortable you can make it now, the more real and inviting to your mind it will be when you seek to return. And you will take refuge here frequently enough for it to become a familiar home.

Like any home that's lived in, this one will evolve and change as your needs change, so nothing is locked in concrete. You have complete power to make changes at any time you choose; remember, you are god of your own inner reality, and what you create, you can re-create as you choose. And you don't even need to lock it when you leave and return to your workaday existence, because it is beyond the reach of anyone else in the whole world.

If you have followed through on all this, you now own something you didn't have just a few minutes ago. Your Shangri-la can be just as perfect, just as subjectively real, as you want it to be. With practice, you will find you can retreat there for mental and physical renewal nearly anytime you have a few free moments, and even though your retreat may seem to be purely imaginary, the personal benefits you can obtain from using it are very real. It will *work* for you, because it is a valid part of your subjective reality.

I hasten to emphasize that I intend no implication of equivalence between this subjective reality and a similar physical reality; obviously there's none. Your Shangri-la presently has no underlying material structure for others to sense and therefore it has no "objective reality." There are both advantages and disadvantages to this: being nonmaterial, there is nothing for others to physically violate or steal, nothing for the government to tax, nothing requiring maintenance and utility expenditures. And any changes you desire can be made free and instantaneously. On the other hand, the absence of materiality that you can see, feel, hear, and smell deprives you of the sensory inputs by which you ordinarily structure and reinforce your subjective images; consequently, you must offset this lack of stimuli with more intense visualization in order to obtain an equally strong subjective reality. And no matter how strong your imagery, you can't physically share your retreat with your friends, or protect yourself from such external manifestations of physicality as rain, extreme temperatures, and screaming mobs.

These distinctions don't invalidate the reality *to you* of your Shangri-la; they only serve to emphasize that there is more than one level of reality and that it is important for you, first, to accept that there *are* nonmaterial realities, and second, to distinguish between them. And to recognize that every man-made physical reality existed first only in the mind of its creator—the architect, inventor, engineer, farmer, chef, etc. Someone's subjective reality is the predecessor of the physical artifact, and your mentally constructed Shangri-la may inspire your construction or acquisition of its physical counterpart at some future time. In the meantime, it's a place where you may spend many moments contemplating the broadened horizons and creative powers that your new understanding of reality brings to you.

Chapter 3

HOW MANY MINDS

I had rather believe all the fables in the legends and in the Talmud and the Alcoran, than that this universal frame is without a mind.

—Francis Bacon
Of Atheism

The nature of reality has been a favorite subject of philosophical speculation ever since there have been philosophers. But if it's true that reality lies in the mind of the beholder, then we may profit from speculating a bit on the nature of the mind itself. Or, as we profess here, the plural: *minds*.

No one questions the existence of the conscious mind, although science has thus far been frustrated in its efforts to explain it solely in terms of the physical brain. This doesn't surprise me at all; having personally experienced what apparently are manifestations of conscious, active minds that are unaware—or unaccepting—of the long-past deaths

26

of their respective physical bodies and of their present discarnate condition, I don't expect science ever to successfully explain the mind in purely physiological terms. If it is true, as it seems, that the consciousness, personality, and memories of an individual can somehow survive the death and decay of the physical brain, then it follows that mind transcends its mortal locus and can never be fully explained in an exclusively material context.

But if the brain isn't the mind, what is it? I liken it to an interface—the pilot's cockpit or cabin, if you will—through which your nonphysical, conscious mind-essence perceives via your normal, physical senses and manipulates your physical body in this temporal reality. A physical or chemical derangement of the brain can disrupt your mental performance, of course, just as a short-circuit or a broken wire in an aircraft pilot's control complex may disable vital instruments or interfere with the flight control. An observer on the ground, seeing a plane flying erratically, might well blame the pilot when in fact a malfunction in the plane's "nervous" system—electrical or hydraulic—is the true cause. Thus it may be with many human mental aberrations: the imperfection may lie in the chemistry, electrical circuitry, or topology of the brain, to the frustration of the mind-essence trying to operate the individual.

If the normal conscious mind represents the pilot, it can operate the vehicle under manual control, but there is at least one alternate means of flight control: the autopilot. An airplane can be maintained in level, steady flight by a nonsentient, computer-like controller that is programmed to react with corrective control adjustments when deviations from the selected altitude, speed, or direction occur. In a sense, this could be considered the plane's "instinct" for sustaining routine progress. It works without judgment. In this respect, the autopilot performs at a "subconscious" level.

But what is the difference between the subconscious and the Superconscious? All phenomena commonly ascribed to the "subconscious" are not in fact attributes of the Superconscious.

Consider, for example, the physiological level: the autonomous nervous system keeps bodily chemistry and metabolism operating in an extremely complex choreography of interactive functions without your conscious attention, and I'm confident that the Superconscious has better things to occupy itself than routine physiological housekeeping. It's conceivable that the physical brain, rather than some level of nonphysical mind, is the operating engineer, but that doesn't satisfy all the observed characteristics of the subconscious. For instance, a "fixed" circuit consisting of established neuronic interconnections in the physical brain should react only to physiological signals, such as responding to the body's oxygen need of the moment by controlling your breathing. Yet you can very easily override the normal action of your lungs by mind alone, merely by directing conscious attention to your breathing. More difficult but possible is conscious control of your heart rate, blood pressure, skin temperature, and probably any other aspect of your biochemistry that normally is on autopilot. This control, I emphasize, is achieved by only your conscious mind. You don't open your skull and physically rearrange your brain cells; you simply override those preprogrammed responses normally performed at some level of inorganic mind beyond or below your normal awareness. In other words, you are consciously overriding not the physical circuitry of your brain, but your *subconscious mind*, that indefinable, nonphysical spark of the universe that is *life*, without which the most marvelous, complex brain or the simplest solitary cell is just so much inert, useless matter.

But there is more to the subconscious than routine sustenance of physical life. All of us have reactive responses to external nonphysical stimuli. These are nonvolitional and often nonrational responses that can't be attributed to simple organic action in the brain when the stimulus is nonphysiological. These responses reveal a *reflexive*, emotional pattern of reaction at some level of mind that is neither conscious nor superconscious.

The ability to develop reflexive, unthinking reactions is essential for coping with physical reality; for example, if you had to consciously perform each motion, in proper sequence, to merely walk across the room, or to speak, or to drive a car, etc., your conscious attention would be so occupied with coordination of the basic physical movements that you'd have no capacity left for productive thought processes. In the process of learning any repetitive function, you *program* your subconscious mind (incidentally reinforcing applicable physical neural circuits) to automatically perform it upon receipt of the appropriate mental stimulus.

Notice that the subconscious mind does only what it is programmed to do, and it does so upon receipt of a triggering stimulus without making any judgment as to whether the response is appropriate to the specific circumstances. If the airplane's autopilot is programmed only to fly straight and level upon command (and lacks more sophisticated sensing facilities), it will do so—right into a mountain standing in its path, if it's not overridden by the human pilot. Just as when you walk across a room, your legs will propel you into the wall in front of you if you don't consciously cue yourself to avoid it. Your subconscious is no more judgmental than a tape recorder; obviously this is not the same level of thinking, judgmental mind as is your ordinary consciousness, let alone your Superconscious.

The most troublesome aspect of the subconscious is psychological, because this level of mind is deeply involved with emotions. An intentional creation of a subconscious "tape recording" may require many conscious repetitions of a nonemotional routine, such as touch-typing, if it is to "play back" reflexively, but a single incident that is accompanied by intense emotion can create a deeply imprinted subconscious response which, under stimulus, will recur repeatedly through the years, long past any relevance to the imprinting incident. Thus the very small child, terrified by having once been locked in a dark closet, may suffer through adulthood with an irrational fear of small rooms. Closed spaces trigger the old tape, even though the

30

childhood incident itself may be long since forgotten, and the fear emotion is regenerated inappropriately. There is no doubt that this sort of thing happens; however, since we perceive the conscious and superconscious minds to be rational—that is, to make intellectually appropriate responses to stimuli—this nonrational, *reactive* process must occur at some other level of mind. We perceive this to be convincing evidence of the existence of a subconscious mind, and it is at this level that the therapist or hypnotist seeks to reprogram ingrained reflexes in his process of rooting out and defusing a patient's irrational phobias, "hang-ups," and various other behavioral eccentricities.

There also is a level of neurological activity wherein response to stimulus is normally performed by nerve circuits in the spinal column, with no intervention at the brain level, but even these seem to be "monitored" at some subconscious level and are subject to modification by cranial-based nerve signals or chemical transmitters. This level of activity often is lumped in with the broad concept of the subconscious; there certainly can be no logic in ascribing these low-level activities to the highly intellectual Superconscious.

On the other hand, it is commonplace in the literature of metaphysics, self-improvement, and hypnosis in particular, to refer to the subconscious mind as the seat of every buried memory, every paranormal ability, even the seat of man's divinity. Paranormal (psychic) abilities are, by definition, not accountable for by what we know of the ordinary, conscious mind—which is a very able instrument in its own right—and it seems absurdly illogical to ascribe such abilities to a nonjudgmental, reactive level of mind that obviously functions on a much lower, nonintellectual level. To the extent that the subconscious is incapable of such things as telepathy, clairvoyance, communication with higher entities, etc., we must ascribe those abilities to the Superconscious.

To delve further into our analogy of the pilot's cabin: should the pilot become weary, he can set the autopilot for a steady course while he disengages from the controls and takes a nap. He can do this with reasonable safety if his plane is equipped with enough sophisticated sensors (radio, radar, altitude, engine troubles, etc.) awake him with an alarm in the event of impending trouble. While this is not approved aviation practice, it corresponds in our analogy to going to sleep and leaving the body to run on autopilot, feeling reasonably secure that in the event of fire, burglary, or other threatening situation, one will awaken in time to take appropriate decisive action.

In an actual airplane, however, there is another choice: a copilot. The copilot's seat permits someone other than the regular pilot to manipulate the plane, so the pilot can relinquish control at his discretion. He may remain in his seat merely to observe, or to forcibly take over the controls should the copilot veer off course or operate the craft inappropriately. On the other hand, if the copilot is a senior pilot of unquestioned integrity and capability, the regular pilot may feel confident in temporarily leaving the control cabin to, say, take a nap in the passenger or cargo compartment.

Something like this is what seems to happen when a "trance reader"[1] goes into an altered state of consciousness and another identity—most commonly, the reader's own Superconscious—manifests by speaking through the reader's vocal apparatus. The conscious mind—the regular pilot—relinquishes control of the communications facilities to another consciousness. When it is the pilot's own Superconscious, it is like a young flier deferring to a senior flight instructor having vastly superior experience and ability, so there is no reason to fear stepping aside temporarily while the senior entity emerges.

There is some difference of opinion among students of metaphysics over how much power the elder statesman—the Superconscious—can bring to bear on influencing the conscious mind. Some believe the Superconscious can override the conscious mind at any time; others believe the conscious mind can, and in most of us usually does, reject and block out even the most urgent efforts of the Superconscious to guide, direct, or warn us.

What this really boils down to is a battle of free

---

[1] A trance reader is a person who, when in trance, serves as a vehicle for verbal communication by what apparently is another level of his/ her own consciousness or, with some readers, that of another entity. The trance may be so light that the reader may not feel at all entranced. He may be fully aware at the normal conscious level, as I usually am when my Superconscious speaks, or he may not know what "he" says until someone tells him later. Among those whose interest brings them into metaphysical-study groups, it appears that about thirty percent can become trance readers.

wills. The Superconscious retains the free will with which it was endowed at the moment of its Spirit creation, while the mortal also is endowed with an independent free will at the conscious level. From this, it seems to follow that the degree of intervention in mortal decisions and actions of which the Superconscious is capable differs markedly from person to person. There are individuals who claim to be completely at the command of their higher selves, despite sometimes violent disagreement on their conscious level; I know others who seem to be completely oblivious to guidance that their higher selves are desperately trying to drive through blocks erected by their conscious-level free will. I admit to no hard and fast rule. Perhaps in this experience we are supposed to learn harmony of our own distinct and essentially discrete wills.

It's probably safe to say that most of us are displaced from the pilot's seat only if we choose to allow our higher self to manifest.[2] As seems to be the rule in metaphysics, there are exceptions to the rule; the literature indicates that certain individuals may be susceptible to hosting manifestations by entities whom they don't invite, at least consciously. There are some simple precautions against intrusions by undesirables that should be practiced

[2] Some individuals can relinquish partial control to entities other than their own superconscious selves; these are trance *mediums*, who may serve as channels for communications with discarnate spirits, or discarnate souls trapped in the physical plane, or the Superconsciouses of living persons. It is our understanding that these "external" sources are allowed to partially control the mortal only with permission of the mortal's own Superconscious, which presumably shields one from entities having possibly nefarious purposes.

by anyone actively engaging in psychic experimentation; some of these will be discussed in later chapters.

So we seem to have at least three levels of mind: subconscious, conscious, and superconscious.[3] These are convenient but broad distinctions, or shadings, rather than totally discrete separations. We are aware of various levels of consciousness, which seem to shade across a broad spectrum of mental-activity levels, as revealed by the electro-encephalograph's tracing of the brain's beta-, alpha-, gamma-, and delta-wave forms. We believe the right-brain and left-brain hemispheres are hosts to different aspects of our conscious thought processes. The subconscious has its own spectrum of obscure levels of activity, while the Superconscious probably has abilities beyond our mortal conception. We can only say with reasonable certainty that the human mind operates at many levels, including some that are superior and some that are inferior to what we consciously think of as our "mind."

---

[3]Characteristics and genesis of the superconscious mind are discussed further in Chapters 5 and 6 and are alluded to throughout this book.

Chapter 4

FAITH BEGINS AT HOME

*There are no whole truths; all truths are half-truths.
It is trying to treat them as whole truths that plays
the devil.*

—Alfred North Whitehead
Dialogues of Alfred North Whitehead

Now that we've stretched the scope of your possibility thinking to include nonmaterial realities and higher minds, we have many realms to explore. But if you came away from the previous chapters with the impression that ascertainment and definition of the absolute nature of *material* reality is difficult, wait until you try to pin down absolutes in other realms! From this ordinary level of physical existence, it seems virtually impossible to describe absolute rules and relationships governing the structures of other levels, and I will not try. This book defines what my experience and sources of information lead me *at this moment* to believe or to suspect is true of certain nonmaterial realms, but you'll find no dogmatic assertions proffered as absolutes. I leave that degree of self-delusionary certainty to those who claim a corner on metaphysical truths, and I would encourage you to insist upon your right to weigh and winnow their assertions and to accept only what you can fit comfortably into your personal reality structure—just as I expect you to do with this book. I believe no mortal is infallible in his knowledge; as for alleged nonmortal sources manifesting psychically, it is my understanding (from allegedly nonmortal sources!) that no psychic is allowed to be a hundred percent accurate. I'll come back to this later.

There may be an infinite assortment of alternate realities, but we are interested here only in those in which we believe sentient beings "reside"[1] and/or interact. There may even be an infinitude of inhabited realms, but perhaps only a few are detectable to us from here.

What kinds of sentient beings might be found in those realms? Your own higher self, for one! In Chapters 1 and 3, I discussed the concept in which each of us physical, mortal beings possesses another level of mind called the Superconscious. This

---

[1] When you are dealing with nonphysical realms and nonphysical inhabitants, there is some question of whether it's appropriate to speak of an entity (ostensibly with no defined body) "residing" in "nothing." Does a mind have boundaries? Can it rest on nothing more substantial than, say, the thought-form of a chair? Perhaps there is some very nebulous counterpart of form in the nonmaterial realities. It's convenient to assume so, anyway, because we on this level don't know how to think and express ourselves in other than terms of physical places and tangible things.

level allegedly is capable of independent thought and of interaction with other entities—discarnate *and* incarnate—operating in those nonphysical realms. This is a very significant concept because, if true, it means you have inherent in yourself an aspect capable of acting directly in those alternate realities. Furthermore, it means that you are not solely reliant for your information on those disembodied entities fitting the popular—and controversial—concept of "souls of the dead."

Now that we've opened the subject of "communicating with the dead," it is necessary to address the commonplace assertion that consorting with Spirits is evil and condemned by God. Fundamentalist sects, in particular, are vociferous in their literal interpretations of those biblical injunctions against seeking communication with the dead—and, for that matter, seeking the services of fortune tellers, wizards, and all psychic practitioners.

Even though many mainstream Western theologies deny the continuity of nonphysical individuality following the transition we call death (and therefore the impossibility of authentic communication with the departed), metaphysical research reveals strong evidence tending to substantiate that continuity. There is negligible doubt in my mind that some sensitive persons *do* upon occasion receive information from discarnate sources of some sort.

Even many fundamentalists accept the reality of manifestations by nonphysical entities other than God and the Angels. In 1 Samuel 28, Saul is confronted by an imminent battle, and he seeks reassurance that the Lord of the Old Testament is

38

behind his cause. However, he and his prophets seem to have lost psychic contact with the Lord, so he seeks a medium, even though his people are forbidden to do so. He is led to a woman who discerns his disguised identity and is fearful of entrapment. Upon his assurances of immunity, she goes into trance and calls up, at Saul's request, the alleged personality of Samuel, who is deceased. The manifesting entity, whose identity Saul accepts as Samuel even though he can't perceive his form, reports the bad news that he (Saul) has fallen into disfavor with the Lord, and then withdraws. We are later told that Saul ultimately was killed by the Lord, for seeking to communicate with the dead, so we can't take this episode as condonement of the practice!

There are many other biblical references warning against communication with the dead. But it seems logical that if it were indeed *impossible* to communicate with the dead, there would be no need to warn the upsophisticated folk of that era against doing so. I have found nothing in the English versions of the biblical account to suggest that Saul was not in fact in touch with a surviving facet of Samuel; the presence of warnings against seeking audience with the dead seems to refute the argument that physical death brings total dissolution of the personality.

The alternative explanation, repeatedly discoursed upon by the late Herbert W. Armstrong[2]

---

[2] For example, see "Communication with the Dead—Is It Possible?" in *Plain Truth* magazine, April, 1983.

and others, is that these manifestations *do* occur, but that all are the work of demons masquerading as personalities of deceased humans. This explanation is used to exact strict adherence to the biblical injunctions against involving one's self in psychic/metaphysical interactions, but overlooks the equally psychic/metaphysical content of numerous other biblical accounts that are accepted as proofs of the supernatural powers of God.

Consider some of the admonitions in Deuteronomy 18 as they are translated into English: "There shall not be found among you any one . . . that useth divination, or an observer of times, or a witch, or a charmer, or a consulter with familiar spirits, or a wizard. . . ." Well, divination is acquisition of secret knowledge by supernatural means, which must encompass most of the revered biblical prophets. Including Daniel, divining the future of Egypt by interpreting the Pharaoh's psychic dreams; and John, writing the entire book of Revelation to report his supernatural visions.

An "observer of times" is an astrologer, which was but one of the talents of the Magi, revered for bringing gifts to the newborn Christ-child and not reviled for being astrologers. *Magi* is the plural of *Magus*, for which one of the meanings is *sorcerer*. Which also could be a "charmer," defined as *enchanter* or *magician*—what Moses appeared to be, when striking water from the rock or turning his walking stick into a serpent. He also could be deemed a "wizard," which is merely another version of *sorcerer* or alternatively, a sage or very wise person. "Witch" is simply the feminine version of *wizard*, both words having a common old English root. And so on.

The intent of this exercise is to point out the duality of attitudes in the Bible regarding those manifestations that today we would ascribe to psychic/metaphysical/paranormal sources: *those that can be construed in support of God's power* (as perceived by biblical writers and various church authorities) *are good; those that can't are abominable.* We are left, then, with a choice: either blindly accede to the authorities' blanket condemnation of all metaphysical involvements; or independently draw our *own* conclusions regarding the divinity or iniquity of each paranormal manifestation we encounter in the present time—that is, to decide for one's self!

While I am among the first to warn newcomers to the field that there certainly are impostors and deceivers among discarnate entities, there are selected manifesting personalities claiming to be individuals I have known exceedingly well in their mortal existences and who display knowledge and personality patterns that I find convincing. I'm doubtful that impostors could deceive so effectively, or that any would even have reason to. And if you accept the premise that a manifesting Spirit may serve as an agent of God, then it's patently inaccurate to insist that all psychic manifestations are the work of demons. Therefore, so long as a Spirit's assertions and activities appear to be positively motivated and are consistent with my own concept of uplifting spiritual direction, I'm willing to accept them for whom they seem to be. And

41

most of them seem to be entities that have previously experienced mortal human life.

This is not to dismiss biblical prohibitions out of hand. There are good reasons for warning the uninitiated against incautiously patronizing every self-styled psychic, since entities of questionable character and motivation *can* manifest, often masquerading as benevolent beings. One of the first lessons the student of metaphysics should learn is that spiritual entities are not all "Spiritual," in the religious sense of the word. In biblical times, it probably was better to warn an unsophisticated population away from *all* psychic phenomena than to risk its falling prey to deceitful entities. Yet paramount among the paranormal happenings related in the Bible is the Resurrection itself, and to label all paranormal endeavors as sinful while simultaneously basing an entire doctrine on the spiritual aspect of historical supernatural events seems to me to be an exercise in sophistry. *I* certainly don't accept the premise that *all* communication with nonphysical entities is evil, or I wouldn't be writing this book. But as with any exploration, discretion is in order.

While we're on the subject of precautions, there is another potential pitfall in the patronizing of psychics: failing to understand that each individual must put faith in his own pathways to inner knowledge above all other sources, many who seek the services of psychic seers are looking for "outside" sources of guidance for every decision. With this motivation, the novice risks entrusting the course of his life to the wrong hands, allowing his deci-

42

sions to be influenced by mortals or nonmortals of unknown and unprovable qualifications. This is a misdirection of faith and an abdication of free will, both of which endanger progress toward personal enlightenment and which are contrary to biblical objectives as well as to mankind's.

An extreme example of misdirection of faith culminated a few years ago in the unfortunate Jonestown episode, in which several hundred individuals elected to commit suicide at the insistence of their cult leader, the late Reverend Jim Jones. It was perhaps doubly unfortunate that many of the victims were children, who were misguided, coerced, or forced into partaking of the suicidal beverage. This tragedy of misplaced faith saddened the world.

Jim Jones once preached positive, enlightening values, but there was that in him which attracted followers who, being either too naive or too lacking in self-confidence to formulate their own, sought a prepackaged theology. There also evidently was that within him which nurtured a God complex, so that he increasingly came to play upon his followers' need for an external object of faith, until he assumed the mantle of absolute authority. Undoubtedly many followers had drifted away earlier, as they became increasingly uncomfortable with Jones's drive toward authoritarianism, leaving a following comprised principally of hapless sheep who had given up all judgment and free will. The rest is dismal history.

If there are any absolute truths, this must be one: *no source is absolute.* No psychic is one hundred percent accurate. No minister nor priest—nor, I daresay, even the Pope—is infallible. No spiritual revelations short of Christ's are too sacred to be questioned, and we can't be certain that His have been accurately recorded. Omniscience is accorded to no man, only to God.

I will be among the first to caution you to evaluate your sources of information and carefully weigh their pronouncements; but you *do* have your own, innate, spiritual source of esoteric knowledge and, if you can't trust your own higher self, then whom can you trust? So, rather than urging you to indiscriminately burn all books of the occult, as some ministers do, I simply recommend ranking your own power of choice above any other's and building your belief structure according to your own criteria. Learn to evaluate your sources and weigh their pronouncements in terms of what you can comfortably accept into your own paradigm.

So it isn't necessary to shun all practicing psychics, but it is necessary to bolster your faith in yourself and to maintain a healthy skepticism of all allegedly psychic revelations—even your own! Your higher sources, like all others, are bound by the rule that no one can be given information that is one hundred percent correct. This may seem arbitrary, capricious, or even unfair, but consider the reason: each of us must eventually learn to draw his own conclusions; to discriminate between wheat and chaff, truth and error, right and wrong, with the mature judgment of his conscious mind. But if you were to find a source of information that was guaranteed to be a hundred percent correct, you'd certainly subordinate your own fallible judgment to that infallible source, thereby failing to achieve the individual growth intended for you in this mortal cycle. Understanding how total accuracy of given information defeats this one goal of the mortal experience makes it clear why revelations of total accuracy are denied to all higher sources, and why it is left to each of us to ascertain which details are compatible with his personal belief structure. So don't be afraid of psychic revelations, but don't accept them beyond question, either. Simply evaluate them and accept or reject as you choose.

Are there any hints to help in this evaluation? Yes, but again you must develop critical approaches that work best for you. For example, a legitimate psychic counselor is able to verbalize guidance he/she receives psychically from *your* Superconscious; guidance that your conscious mind has—for whatever reason—been blocking from you. The psychic may be aware of this source and tell you as much, or he/she may tell you that the communication comes from your "Spirit Guide." Other psychics may not themselves realize the source of this information, attributing it to their own "powers," or their "guides," or perhaps even to God.

If the source is indeed your own Superconscious, even though the information may be at odds with your conscious beliefs and expectations, and even though you know it may fall short of total accuracy, you can nevertheless feel a "comfortableness," a compelling sense of "rightness" with it. Conversely, a figurative red flag of caution raised somewhere in the depths of your mind is a good indication that the source is not your higher self and that the information is erroneous, distorted, or even intentionally deceitful, regardless of its proclaimed source. If you will preserve your right—and obligation to yourself—to make your own free-will evaluations of all the information you encounter, you will avoid falling victim to someone else's misguidance, whether it be inadvertent or intentional.

Another yardstick for measuring psychically gleaned information is, perhaps surprisingly, *logic*. Does this new information make sense? Is it reasonable? Is it compatible with other information at hand? Does it explain something heretofore inexplicable?

In this regard, it's important to realize that what seems improbable in the context of our material concepts may in fact be perfectly logical in the nonphysical realms, and that something which seems incredible is not necessarily illogical. The logicality of an element is a measure of how well it fits into and complements its surrounding reality structure, not how incongruous it may seem out of context.

It also seems valid to suppose that our mortal rules of logic are parallel to those on other levels; if in fact we are counterparts of our higher selves, it presumably follows that we share a common structure of intellectual logic. If this is correct, we are justified in examining the logical acceptability of information from allegedly learned sources as one measure of its validity.

The world is full of those, including many well-intentioned clergymen, who believe theirs is the absolute, complete, and unalterable truth, and they will urge, coax, cajole, and perhaps threaten you to adopt their structure, down to the minutest detail, without question—lest you suffer dire consequences! But to accede to these demands is to subvert your free-will decisions for the sake of accommodating another's reality; to confine your horizons for growth to the limits of another's closed box of concepts; to literally *bestow your very faith upon another mortal*. Conversely, so long as you are selective, you are exercising faith in yourself and your inner guidance.

This, then, is the key to accommodation of *any* self-proclaimed source of higher knowledge: accept that with which you are comfortable in your own reality and logic structures, and hold in abeyance that with which you are not. (I say to hold in abeyance, rather than to discard, because you may later wish to examine it again. Personal growth sometimes puts previously untenable concepts in a more acceptable light, just as it renders some old favorites no longer satisfactory.)

If you keep foremost in mind that personal enlightenment occurs only within yourself; that pathways acclaimed by others are to be accepted or rejected as your own inner guidance elects; that *you*—and no other—are responsible for your reality structure and your resulting actions; you will not abdicate your freedom of choice by blind acceptance of another's dogma.

And neither will you demand that others blindly accept yours. You will be neither cult follower nor cult leader, and you will never become a puppet of mortals or of psychically manifesting entities. To the extent that you must think and act on faith, it will be on faith in your own inner values and, if you're so inclined, faith in your own concept of God. Just as I exhort you to do, I have picked and chosen from the teachings of many others to arrive at the reality structure I profess here; I certainly did *not* originate most of the concepts in this book. Much of its foundation is adapted from the dissertations of Astar, the prime spiritual mentor for Bruce Born's Jupiter Movement, and from the voluminous legacy of psychic information channeled by this century's best-documented psychic, Edgar Cayce. The superstructure has been formed from firsthand observation of several psychics, including my wife, Marianne, and from various discarnate sources. You can meet these teachers—"Our Gang"—in the Afterword of this book

Chapter 5

GETTING INTO
THE SPIRIT

*A little philosophy inclineth a man's mind to athe-
ism, but depth in philosophy bringeth men's minds
about to religion.*

—Francis Bacon
Of Atheism

Now it's time to get serious about this business
of nonphysical realities and nonmortal beings that
I've been alluding to in the previous four chapters.
Is there in fact something beyond this temporal,
physical existence that you can reasonably incorporate into your personal reality? Certainly the major religions of the world insist that there is, and
their adherents at least pay lip service to some concept of higher levels of intellect and existence. On
the other hand, the last two centuries of research
by physical scientists seem, in the eyes of many,
to have disproven so many church-propagated beliefs that it has become unfashionable in modern

Western society to profess—or even admit to—a belief in the unseen.

This book is not about religions, but it does deal with alternate realms of human existence. The premise of this chapter is that you do in fact have an aspect of existence that transcends the apparent, mortal one; that you do have a Spirit, and that the higher mind of your Spirit is your Superconscious. There is a wealth of empirical evidence to support this contention, although it is true that we have not yet confirmed this transcendent aspect of existence in the scientific laboratory.

And it may be that we never will. The scientific lab examines details of the physical, three-dimensional, and mortal universe, seeking to define objectively the external absolutes of this perceived reality. The devices used to examine the aspects of that reality are *of* that reality; i.e., the physical sensory organs of scientists are assisted by instruments fashioned of physical matter—microscopes, particle accelerators, computers, etc.—using physical energies such as light, X-rays, and electronic signals. In other words, the scientific exploration of physical reality is performed with tools derived from that reality and which therefore are responsive to it. But we have no compelling reason to suppose that tools derived from physical reality should be responsive to occurrences in some other reality (although it would certainly be sheer good fortune if they were), so the alleged failure of scientists using these tools to detect other realities with the consistency that physical science demands does not *dis*prove their existence. Nor does it prove their nonexistence, since it is logically impossible to prove a negative.

To explore any realm, one must have access to it and the tools to detect occurrences within it. But, as the only element of physical reality to claim perception of other realms, mortal man becomes the sole known instrument in the obvious universe through which we can explore those other realms. It seems unfortunate for the scientific-minded that the single "detector" we have can return only subjective information, for this never will convince the skeptic bystander.

Neither will it give us absolutely accurate, objective information or precisely repeatable experiments. So long as we are limited to human perception and interpretation of those other realms, the information we compile will be filtered through the individual subjective faculties of the perceivers, and we will be unable to define absolutes. However, just as our inability to define absolutes in our familiar physical world doesn't keep us from describing and using a workable, if illusory, practical reality, we can arrive at some workable conclusions concerning some of the alternate realities.

You will recall from earlier chapters that our supposedly "objective" physical reality is an illusion of consensus; that its apparent form and function are mutually agreed upon by most perceivers. If only two persons in the whole world perceived a tabletop to be solid while it was transparent to everyone else, we might be justified in supposing those two individuals were hallucinating, hoaxing, or irrational. The same can be said of reported pa-

51

ranormal experiences: if a given alleged occurrence is reported only rarely and by very small numbers of percipients, we may be justified in doubting the underlying "objective" reality of those perceptions. But if hundreds of individuals report paranormal experiences that share one or more common elements among their individual uniquenesses (subjectivities), a reasonable researcher surely is justified in suspecting that there is some reality behind those common elements. Its absolute nature may be quite different from the reported perceptions, but *something* must be at the root of those common experiences. If that something won't fit into our accepted reality, it must signify a need to modify our concepts. Any culture tends to resist modifying its consensus "truth" structure until vastly overwhelming evidence forces it to do so, but we have seen earlier that each of us is free to modify his personal reality as his growing knowledge dictates.

Newcomers to the study of metaphysics are often overcome by the sheer mass of literature revealing the paranormal, subjective experiences of individuals from all historical eras and geographical locations. While it is easy—and proper—to be skeptical of each *individual* reported experience, it seems unreasonable and perhaps even irrational to summarily reject the threads common to many thousands just because they are in disagreement with present scientific knowledge. Although it may be true that no single experience can be objectively substantiated beyond doubt, the laws of probability strongly imply some absolute, undefined reality underlying those perceptions that are common to many reported experiences.

Among the common elements reported in the mass of anecdotal literature are such controversial things as mental telepathy, near-death experiences, perceptions of future events, out-of-body experiences, memories of previous lives, demonic possession, apparitions, and many other subjective phenomena that are unaccountable within the framework of our perceived physical universe. I will not recount instances of these experiences in convincing quantities; if you wish to review them, such authors as Shirley MacLaine, Ian Stevenson, Elisabeth Kubler-Ross, Harold Puthoff and Russell Targ, Edith Fiore, John Keel, Ivan Sanderson, Brad Steiger, Jess Stearn, Ruth Montgomery, Jean Dixon, and countless others will launch you into this world of personal accounts and speculative ruminations. I mention the literature here only to give a hint of the quantity of published evidence of esoteric subjective experiences. And it's barely a hint; there are literally thousands of books on supersensible realities.

Recalling the definition of personal reality as a belief that works for you, we can conclude that some of these paranormal experiences are indeed real to their perceivers. When a telepathic communication brings aid to one in dire need, it *works*. When a near-death experience gives its perceiver a new, less fearsome attitude toward death in all its inevitability, it *works*. If the apparition of a departed loved one brings consolation and comfort to the bereaved, it *works*. These, then, *are* personal realities to the individuals involved, and you can accommodate them within your own reality framework as you choose, even if you never directly experience any of them. But our interest here goes deeper: is there some underlying absolute but alternate reality implied by these experiences that we may beneficially explore? Do these subjective experience indicate that some component of every human being is capable of operating in that alternate reality? In a word, yes. That's the premise of this book.

A common religious viewpoint of man perceives him to be comprised of body, mind and soul, with the soul representing a nonphysical essence that may survive mortality. In this concept, the relationship of the soul to the other components often is vaguely defined. Is the soul an ethereal entity capable of thought and volition that is independent of the conscious mind? Or is it only a "spiritual" counterpart of the physical body, sharing the consciousness and personality of the mortal individual? Is it a creation of the mortal, having had no existence before the physical host was conceived, or has it existed independently and will it continue to do so after death? Does it exert any influence on the mortal—or vice versa? Is there a difference between "soul" and "Spirit"?

This book makes a distinction between those two words, reserving "soul" for that aspect of the mortal that some call the "etheric body," and which will be discussed in context later on. What we are principally concerned with is called "Spirit" throughout the book. In our context, the *Spirit is you*. You—the real you—are much more than a physical, flesh-and-blood creature with a temporal conscious mind. Your physical body is not you, it is a minor aspect of you; a vehicle with which to interact with the rest of the physical universe during this experience. Your brain is not you; it is only the bio-electronic control center through which your mind operates your body and receives your sensory impressions. The real you is a Spirit; a nonmaterial, sentient entity created in a nonmaterial reality and far more active in the unseen world than your conscious mind is aware of.

How's that again? More active on other levels than you're conscious of? If this is true, there must be a component of your Spirit that thinks, acts, and reacts independently of your conscious mind! Your superconscious mind.

Edgar Cayce proclaimed the existence in each Spirit—that includes each human—of an exalted mind of which the mortal, conscious mind normally is not aware. To distinguish this higher mind, he called it the *Superconscious*. This higher, "hidden" mind is an attribute of man not commonly included in the religious stereotype of the "soul," but it is a fundamentally vital concept in this book's effort to enlarge your structure of personal reality. It has become an accepted part of my personal reality through several years of having the opportunity to discern the manifestations, through various individuals, of activities that are satisfactorily explained by the existence of the Superconscious, and by observing some of the ways that their Superconsciouses appear to function within unseen realms.

55

In short, the concept works for me, and one of the ways in which it works is by providing a viable mechanism to explain most paranormal phenomena.

According to the concepts being developed here, everyone has a superconscious mind.[1] So let's examine the nature of yours in a little more detail: your Superconscious has intellect, the power to reason. It has memory. It has free will—which sometimes will conflict with your conscious free will! It has opinions, which likewise may conflict with your consciously formed ones. It has awareness, apparently on several levels. It has emotions. It has a personality. It forms attachments to other spiritual entities. It has amassed knowledge. It has goals, and the ability to act toward fulfilling them.

In fact, your superconscious mind is quite similar to your aware, conscious mind. More accurately, vice versa; your mortal, conscious mind can be thought of as a somewhat isolated extension of your Superconscious. The two parts seem to be linked by a communication channel that allows a free flow of data from conscious to Superconscious, but which restricts the flow (usually for good if not obvious reaons) from Superconscious to conscious.

The superconscious mind is the seat of many observed abilities and characteristics, such as hyp-

---

[1] Metaphysical writers don't agree on capitalization of terms for revered entities. Is it *superconscious*, or *Superconscious*? Some of our higher sources, when manifesting via automatic writing, always capitalize *Superconscious* and *Spirit* when used as nouns; as adjectives, they may not be capitalized (superconscious mind; spirit realm).

notic recall, that are more popularly attributed to the "subconscious" mind. There is nothing either *sub*ordinate or *sub*servient about the Superconscious, however; it is in all respects superior to the conscious mind and is much more fittingly identified as Superconscious.

Don't lose sight of the fact that we are talking about an integral aspect of *you*, not some unrelated entity. Your Spirit, with its superconscious level of mind, is the real you. It is temporarily utilizing a mortal body—yours—and has split off a part of its intellect for your conscious awareness, interaction and reaction, and consequent growth during the physical experience. Your subconscious mind is just a primitive bridge between the animal instinct inherited by the physical body and your reflexive mental reactions, serving most beneficially as autopilot in control of the countless bodily functions that would consume far too much attention were you required to perform them consciously.

Your Spirit is sometimes said to have an ethereal body, or an astral body,[2] that resides within your physical body. This probably is said largely to help us to visualize a locale for the Spirit in familiar three-dimensional concepts. In levels of existence other than this material one, space, time, and di-

_____

[2] Terminology for the nonphysical realms is about as vague and indistinct as the wraiths alleged to inhabit them. Some will insist that "The Spirit has an ethereal body, while the soul has an astral body," thus creating several distinctions that are really understood only by the individual proclaiming them. There undoubtedly is much under the ethereal sun that we do not dream of, but sufficient unto this point in our discourse is the uncertainty of the inevitable, let alone that of the evitable!

mension are inexpressible in terms that we can comprehend with our conscious-mind framework of reality, and probably the most universally agreed-upon characteristic of the higher realms is that what we know as time is indeterminate there.

In fact, how do you define *there* in a realm without physical boundaries, structures, and measurable coordinates? Do discarnate Spirits live "there"? Does *your* Spirit live "there," or does it literally reside in your body and somehow extend itself into these other realms?

I believe it is more accurate to say that your Spirit's *focus of attention* is centered in your mortal existence, since it can be shown that your Superconscious's *awareness and ability to manifest* your Spirit's image ranges instantaneously to wherever in the physical world it pleases, and it probably is erroneous to ascribe either form or location to a Spirit. It nevertheless is convenient to think of your Spirit as residing within your body, since its actual configuration is immaterial, anyway. It is the *function* and *purpose* of the Spirit, not the form, that we strive to understand.

If it's true that you really are a Spirit, an inescapable question arises: how did this come about? Is the Spirit life form a consequence of the presumed progress of evolution, having started as a nonsentient organism in the primeval sea and developed through countless chance mutations to an intellect that transcends the very materiality that gave it life? Nothing in Darwin's hypothesis can support this; he couldn't even account for the physical aspect of man to his satisfaction. To suppose

58

that spirit consciousness evolved as a by-product of man's undirected physical evolution is, in my opinion, simply untenable. No dedicated evolutionist has room in his personal reality structure for man to possess a Spirit; no student of metaphysics whose studies have convinced him of the Spirits' reality can wholly accept the concept of evolution as it is taught.

Since the whole premise of this book is centered on the existence of the higher mind of the Spirit and the ways in which it may manifest in support of this premise, we are stuck here with the scientifically unpopular alternative of a nonphysical, sentient aspect of man whose existence is independent of earthly evolution; one which evidently functions in realms that are independent of time and space. This we call Spirit Man, the real you. Each is unique; there are at least as many Spirits as there are mortal humans existing.

But where did these Spirits come from, if they did not evolve from the material universe? We can speculate that each came into existence spontaneously from nothing more than raw, undifferentiated energy—as indeed the physical universe is believed by many to have been converted from energy in the instant of the Big Bang; in this event, where did the Spirits' sentience and intellect come from? Or was (is) there an even higher-order Intellect that created them all from Itself according to a master plan, replicating within each in diminished scale Its own intellect and creative powers?

Viewing the first of these hypotheses in terms of our mortal understanding, the spontaneous creation of billions of similar spirits—an ethereal *genus*, so to speak—as random products of exploding, mindless energy surpasses the limits of probability, implying as many billions of miracles as there were Spirits created. The alternative hypothesis requires the admittedly inexplicable existence of one God, capable of creating from Itself a host of lower-order beings replicating in diminished measure Its omniscient and omnipotent characteristics. In the conventional view, such powers are inherent with God, so the latter hypothesis requires but a single miracle: the existence of God. Plain old mortal-style logic points strongly to the single miracle as being the more probable.

So is there a God, despite the efforts of science to prove Him unnecessary to our reality? Is there really a Master Plan for the universe, conceived and administered by a Master Executive? While confirmation of the existence of Spirits would support the affirmative, let's try a little more basic logic.

Consider the topics of *intricacy* and *chance*. If we assume there was no plan, no directing influence, no God-mind at work in the evolution of our physical world, it would follow that everything—including you and I—is a product of chance. But we, in just our mortal aspects, are indescribably intricate; so much so that several centuries of intense research by biological scientists have barely scratched the surface of the incredibly complex interactions that occur with exquisite delicacy of control in our bodies. We don't even know yet just how an individual's body cells, all identical in their genetic heritage and DNA codes, differentiate exactly as needed to form hundreds of unique, specialized tissues, organs, and structures in the body; yet this is an elementary step in the formation of anything more complex than an amoeba. Can we possibly believe that the perfectly interlocking intricacy of higher living forms occurred through chance and natural selection alone?

To examine the argument of design versus chance, I'm going to move down the scale for a moment to the inanimate level: the Empire State Building was the pride of New York City in the 1930s; a massive monument to man's material creativity that stood unchallenged as the world's tallest building for many years. Constructed of many different materials in thousands of shapes, it was conceived and put together to form a singular, functional edifice. The skeleton, the plumbing, the heating and air conditioning, the electrical and communications circuits, the elevators—all had to be designed and constructed to interact smoothly and in concert to meet the functional requirements of the structure.

If you were to somehow put all the basic materials necessary to build an Empire State Building into an immense basket, shake it up, and dump it out to see if by chance it fell into the form of a complete and fully functional Empire State Building, I contend that you could do so every minute for longer than the age of the universe without obtaining so much as a single complete floor, let alone the hundred-plus contained in the whole building. I leave it to the statisticians to determine how many components of such a building can combine in how many mega-billions of ways, and the probability of their falling at random into an integrated, functional combination; but it seems safe to say that the Empire State Building would have an essentially zero probability of forming by chance.

In fact, this kind of experiment goes on continuously in nature. The near-hundred naturally occurring physical elements of the universe are manufactured from primordial hydrogen by the nuclear-fusion furnaces we call stars. Our sun is a star, a factory of physical elements. It's had a few billion years and incredible energy resources to cause the chance combination of those elements into structured creations; yet we have no evidence that even so much as a doghouse, let alone an Empire State Building, ever has formed on the sun—or anywhere in our solar system. The fact of the matter is that, left to time and chance, highly differentiated matter degrades toward homogeneous undifferentiation. Left abandoned long enough, the Empire State Building will become a mass of rubble in which the original specializations of structures will disappear. The scientific laws of entropy decree that time and chance, in the absence of directed counter influences, will degrade differentiated matter to an ultimate state of inert uniformity.

If billions of years and virtually unlimited supplies of energy and elements don't produce intricate inanimate structures by chance, how much less probable is the chance creation of vastly more intricate living creatures, in multiple thousands of species, on a single planet? Indeed, for this to occur by chance alone would, I believe, be a monumental miracle in itself!

The creation of something new from existing materials begins with *thought*. The architect of the Empire State Building created it in his mind before he drew it on paper. The actual construction, the physical creation, was performed by others, to be sure, but the architect's mind was the prime creator, conceiving the union of money, raw materials, energy, and labor that became the Empire State Building. Using similar ingredients, he also created numerous other buildings having different forms and functions but common components. Today we have countless millions of buildings on this planet, but not a single one has grown by chance. Each and every one was first created in someone's mind and, as buildings grew in complexity from the rudimentary hovel to modern monstrosities with all the facilities of a complete city, their evolution was *directed* by their conceptualizers.

Then if chance can't account for our intricate physical life forms, we are led to realize that there must have been a *mind* at work from the earliest beginnings of life on earth—long before it was inhabited by any physical creature having a mind. Surely there were planning and direction behind the "chance" mutations leading life up its evolutionary scale to a creature suitable as a mortal vehicle for Spirits desiring to partake of the physical experience. Quite simply, it must have been the plan and direction of God the Architect, assisted perhaps by His Spirit minions, that developed physical life on this planet and guided that life into its multitude of expressions, including what we perceive to be the ultimate one to date: physical man.

So, to explain the observed products of *guided* evolution, we postulate the existence of God. Whether you prefer to visualize God anthropomorphically as *He*,[3] as a Universal or Collective Consciousness, or as a nebulous but sentient and directed Prime Force or Energy is a matter of your choice. There is no way, with our mortal limitations of concept, to understand the absolute nature of an Entity so universally pervasive, so awesomely omnipotent, so exaltedly omniscient as God—if He exists—must be. In the words of the Apocrypha: "Ye cannot find the depth of the heart of man, neither can ye perceive the things that he thinketh: then how can ye search out God, that hath made all these things, and know His mind, or comprehend His purpose?"[4]

Though we fail to discern the absolute, we may logically deduce a few of God's characteristics if we assume that human logic is applicable on a cosmic scale. The first and most obvious attribute is *intellect*. We have seen that any creation begins with thought; if our physical universe is in fact a creation, it certainly required an Intellect to create it first in thought.

---

[3] I customarily refer herein to God as "He" not only because of tradition and habit, but for convenience in writing. In doing this, I don't mean to imply that mine is an anthropomorphic concept of God, and I certainly don't mean to be sexist. I perceive the form of the Godhead to be inscrutable within our mortal concepts, and the Creator of all things must possess the attributes of both sexes. Of course there can be no sex in the physical sense in a nonphysical realm.
[4] Judith VII 14.

Another obvious attribute is *purpose*. Nothing is created without a purpose, even if that purpose is nothing more than self-amusement. We may never discern God's purpose, but the very existence of His physical creation is ample evidence that He has one.

The existence of God's purpose immediately establishes something that many persons fail to grasp: *if God has purpose, it inexorably follows that God has standards of right and wrong.* To wit: that which furthers His purpose is right; that which opposes it is wrong. The divine judgment of right or wrong is that simple—and that absolute.

To demonstrate this principle at the mortal level, assume you have a plan for building a house. Subordinate workmen are assisting you and, being capable of independent thought and free-will actions, these workmen make certain decisions about the way they implement your plan. From your viewpoint, those of their decisions and actions that contribute to the planned features and timely completion of the house are right, while those that detract from it or delay its completion are wrong. Thus it would seem to be between man and his superior, God: those activities of man that are in accord with the plan (will) of God are right (good), but those that are inimical to it are wrong (evil). This refutes the concept taught by some who believe that God is merely some Cosmic Creative Energy that is innately neutral—that is just "there," with no intellect, no plan, no direction; and that "good" and "evil" are only relative valuations devised by man and subject to change as man chooses. This dangerous misunderstanding implies that man has no accountability to God; in other words, that man has no role in the Cosmic scheme. The undeniable fact that man exists, and the logical conclusion that man is the product of a Higher, Cosmic intellect fails to support the concept of a neutral God.

The three characteristics of God deduced thus far—intellect, purpose, and absolute standards of right and wrong—appear to be self-evident conclusions of our exercise in speculation. Additional attributes can be postulated with less confidence, perhaps, but nevertheless with high probability when they are seen to explain other perceived aspects of nonphysical realms. For the moment, let's assume that the "mind" of God functions very much as yours and mine do, albeit on an incomprehensibly greater scale. The tentative conclusions that we reach under this assumption may find verification later.

If you can picture yourself as being the only intellect in a vast universe, you'll appreciate how God might have reacted in that same situation sometime in the far distant past: with feelings of utter loneliness. What is the use of absolute dominion over your personal universe if you have no one with whom to share it? No one to share your plans and aspirations, to help you in your creative activities, and to share with you in their benefits? A truly lonely man will find the hovel and the castle equally lonely.

Even the symbolic Adam, blessed with dominion over all of the earth, was given symbolic Eve for the expressed purpose of companionship and sharing of Paradise. Evidently God understands the innate need of an intellect for companionship and interaction with its own kind; an understanding born from His own experience. Thus we logically conclude that another characteristic of God is a *need for companionship*.

But if you are the only intellect in the entire universe, a cosmic mating yell or a celestial phone call won't bring you a companion. Your alternative, if you happen to be omnipotent, is to *create* companions as you desire. All it requires, if you happen to be omnipotent, is a thought!

So you create, first, a single companion. An entity distinct from yourself, composed of whatever ethereal "matter" your own being is made of and given a detached, individually conscious segment of your own intellect. And because that intellect is at first merely a small replica of your own, and because a mere intellectual clone cannot provide the give-and-take required of an effective companion, you give this created being a free will, so that in time it will evolve its own unique personality and become a true companion. And thus your first-born "son" is brought into existence.

According to Edgar Cayce, the prime universal Intellect desired companionship, and so we postulate that God created from Himself the First-Born, a distinct Spirit entity whose consciousness is centered on a "corpuscle" of God but is endowed with free will, and whose power in the universe is comparable with but subordinate to that of God.

At the instant of creation, the "personality" of

67

this First-Born was identical to that of God; he was not yet unique. Just as a single drop of water contains the identical proportions of salts and minerals as are found in its parent ocean, so was the Son's consciousness an exact replica of God's, from whence it came.

The uniqueness of a personality comes, in part, from the individual's experiences. And so the First-Born was sent alone on a "tour" of God's universe, to directly experience its vastness and to observe the ongoing physical creation set in motion by the Father. As he moved about (directed the focus of his awareness) among the far-flung galaxies of the macrocosm and the subatomic universes of the microcosm, he probably participated in directing some aspects of that creation. If the initial seeds of physical life were then in existence, he may himself have manipulated some of the ordered mutations leading that life up the evolutionary scale of complexity.

And he, too, found himself lonely in the vastness of infinity. So, upon his "return" to God, the First-Born urged the Father to create many additional Spirits to participate in His plan while engaging in fellowship with one another. And God, perceiving the First-Born's developed individuality, was satisfied with His experiment in Spirit creation and proceeded with His plan to populate the many realms of His endless domain. In the blink of a cosmic eye, there were created billions of Spirits, each endowed with a "corpuscle" of the mind of God—a single drop from the ocean of His intellect as the nucleus of its individual consciousness—and each potentially as powerful and as righteous as the First-Born, yet forever subordinate to him.[5] *And one of those Spirits is you!*

---

[5] "There is a Spirit in man: and the inspiration of the Almighty giveth them understanding." Job 32:8.

Chapter 6

YOUR STILL SMALL VOICE

> *But the Lord was not in the wind: and after the wind an earthquake; but the Lord was not in the earthquake:*
> *And after the earthquake a fire; but the Lord was not in the fire: and after the fire a still small voice.*
>
> —I Kings 19:11, 12

Of course you're skeptical. Rightly and understandably so. If every human really is a Spirit endowed with a God-consciousness, why is our history a continuum of conflict, turmoil, and mayhem? Where is that God-consciousness evidenced in human affairs? And why aren't we all aware of it in our mortal consciousness? These certainly are valid questions. Major portions of this book are devoted to exploring some of the answers.

The fact that we ordinarily have no direct awareness of a God-consciousness does indeed complicate the human condition. Your God-consciousness resides in the superconscious aspect of your Spirit, which normally is shielded from your conscious perception. While it appears to be an unreasonable obstacle, we are given to understand that this shield is in fact necessary to the very purpose of your mortal experience. To understand this requires examination of that purpose.

Why, do you suppose, would your Spirit, with its ability to transcend the limitations of time and space, elect in the first place to be "confined" in a mortal being having an isolated consciousness that is not cognizant of its (your) higher existence? For that matter, why enter a mortal phase at all?

When an entity is in nonmaterial form, physical reality can be perceived, but not fully participated in. Perhaps it can be likened to the difference between the vicarious experience of seeing a movie of some episode and being a living participant in that same episode. An entity must enter a mortal phase to experience the physical pleasures and exhilarations, as well as the pains and infirmities, of the flesh.

But you can genuinely participate as a mortal being *only if you perceive yourself to be mortal.* If you brought to this life full conscious knowledge of your nonphysical origin and your eons of experience, you couldn't possibly feel yourself to be an innate part of this reality. You cannot fully engage in a culture to which you are a transitory visitor; a society of self-aware Spirits merely wearing physical bodies would more closely resemble patrons of a costume ball than participants in a total experience of the

71

mortal condition.[1] So each superconscious mind isolates a segment of itself to serve as the conscious mind of the physical human, which then starts from zero and grows in awareness and knowledge through the mortal experience. The corpuscle of God-consciousness and the eons of experience that reside in the Spirit's superconscious mind aspect and which predate the physical incarnation ordinarily are shielded from the mortal's awareness. Penetrating this barrier between consciousness levels is one of the goals sought by students of metaphysics.

We understand this isolation of mind-aspects within a Spirit to be highly unilateral. Your superconscious mind is said to be totally aware, at all times, of the content and activities of your conscious mind, but the converse certainly isn't true, at least for most of us. In mechanistic terms, this is like a master computer having full access to the memory content and local activity of a lesser, subsidiary computer, but denying access by the smaller one to most data in the master.

Notice that key word *most*. In actual master/subsidiary computer configurations, the lesser machine has access to that data in the master computer for which it has a legitimate need, and it also probably receives some degree of direction from the master, even though it may be only at periodic intervals or

[1] According to Cayce and others, Spirits in one era did in fact "wear" physical forms while retaining their full awareness and some found the experience so pleasurable that they became addicted to certain pleasures of physicality and neglected to evolve upward as planned. So the rules were changed to separate physical-level awareness from spiritual-level awareness and to impose finite limits on the duration of any given physical sojourn, which established mortality.

at times of uncommon need. The same appears true, to greatly varying degrees in different individuals, of the conscious-mind relationship to the Superconscious. You very likely receive occasional signals from your Superconscious, although you may not recognize them as such, because they seem indistinguishable from your ordinary conscious thoughts, feelings, and reactions.

For most of us, the subtlety of these higher-source signals is necessitated by the need to perceive one's self as a creature of conscious decisions, which indeed one is. Your conscious free will easily can override an impulse from your Superconscious, so long as you don't distinguish that impulse from ordinary conscious thought. It also *can* override it even if you are aware of its source, but the very knowledge of its "higher" origin is likely to inhibit your exercise of free will. So for most of us, the Superconscious keeps a very low profile, because learning to self-discipline free will is one of the major lessons we're to master in this physical experience.

There are other intended lessons, too, which vary greatly among different individuals but which each Superconscious is bound to impose. Because of this, your Superconscious may gently nudge you from time to time, but this in no way diminishes the validity of the physical experience so long as you respond to those impulses according to your own conscious free will.

There are individuals, however, who have developed sufficiently to take in stride the conscious knowledge of a higher self; who can use that knowledge to enhance, rather than to invalidate, their mortal experience. These persons will be led to seek evidence of their superconscious mind's existence and activities. The fact that you have read this far into this book strongly suggests that you are one of these. If so, you must be wondering what to look for; how to recognize spiritual input. In the rest of this chapter, we'll be examining some approaches for you to try.

The Superconscious (which we will call "SC" for short) usually employs the easiest and least obvious method to "get through." Of course this varies greatly from person to person. Probably the most common way is to plant thoughts in the conscious mind that are perceived as ordinary conscious thoughts. Another method is through intuition or hunches. Or it may be the still, small voice commonly ascribed to conscience.

Some persons experience physical reactions, such as inexplicable visceral discomfort upon encountering certain individuals or situations. Or dreams may occasionally be used to communicate, perhaps at a subliminal or symbolic level, although genuine "message" dreams are less frequent than some dream interpreters claim. There are sensitive individuals who receive visions, like dreaming while awake. Or detect aromas. Or hear spoken messages (not *all* of those institutionalized for hearing voices are insane!). Beyond these manifestations, there are many "tools" used by those experienced in one aspect or another of metaphysics which help them to receive information from other levels of existence, such as the pendulum, crystal ball, Ouija board, and others.

Your own Superconscious no doubt has employed one or more of these ways to communicate with the conscious "you" on more occasions than you suppose. Just think back: have you ever had a "thought out of the blue," a hunch that turned out to be correct, a good or bad "gut reaction," or a vivid and seemingly meaningful dream? Something that you can't fully ascribe to your conscious, rational thought processes, yet which proved to be accurate? Flimsy evidence, perhaps, but many such incidents in your life *may* have been communication from your Superconscious.

Now that you've been exposed to the concept, you can be alert to future incidents of possible communication (*psychic input*, in the jargon of metaphysics), analyze them, and come to a tentative conclusion as to whether they seem to originate beyond your conscious mind. There probably will be a high uncertainty factor, because most of us don't receive input neatly labeled as being of superconscious origin, but over a period of time you may become increasingly aware of guidance or impulses not fully accountable for by your conscious-mind activities.

This passive waiting for your Superconscious to reveal itself convincingly can prove both time-consuming and frustrating, and you may wish to try a more active search. This, too, may prove inconclusive, but if you don't try, you'll never know, will you? So let me challenge your sense of adventure by suggesting that you try initiating a dialogue with your higher self! You can't lose more than a few minutes a day in the effort.

The most common technique for inviting your Superconscious to manifest is the practice of meditation. You may already be engaging regularly in one of the many forms of meditation, and you may consequently already have been in touch with your Superconscious but ascribed its manifestations to something or someone else.

There is nothing mysterious or even slightly hazardous about meditation. It is essentially a procedure to relax both body and conscious mind to the deepest degrees possible, thereby clearing a channel through which higher sources may be more readily perceived. If you followed through on the Shangri-la experiment in Chapter 2, you already have performed a relaxation exercise that is suitable for meditation. Other meditation routines are equally valid; if you already have adopted one particular method—and it works for you—then by all means stick with it.

Relaxing the body first entails cessation of all voluntary muscular activity and then relieving muscular tensions and other little discomforts and tactile awarenesses through conscious effort. Having eliminated the demands placed on your attention by your body, so that you are essentially oblivious to physical sensations, you next strive to clear your mind of the profusion of thoughts that are poised on its periphery, ready to leap into the spotlight of mental attention. This idling of the mind—not thinking at all—is extremely difficult for most of us to achieve, and it may require many sessions of practice. Some schools of meditation recommend a chant, or *mantra*, intended to give your mind a repetitious, uncomplicated focus of attention that requires no real thought but closes out those lurking, stray thoughts that always seem ready to clamor for attention and distract you from the state you are striving to achieve. A chant may serve this purpose, but for some of us, at least, it also tends to obscure input from the Superconscious, which often is nebulous at best. I feel it is preferable to have your mind totally quiet, envisioning perhaps a large, empty area in the center of your consciousness; the inevitable wisps of thought milling about the edges can be held at bay by mentally ignoring them as much as possible. When you have arrived at a psychically conducive state, an electroencephalograph would show that your biologically generated brain waves have slowed in frequency to what the medical profession labels the *alpha* rhythm (or, for some persons, even slower), signifying an altered state of consciousness.

If you don't already have a favorite relaxation technique, you might try the one included in Chapter 14 of this book. You can familiarize yourself with it and try it alone, but there is a distinct advantage to having a partner lead you through the steps. (In fact, a partner usually is an asset in all your experimental research into the existence and nature of things metaphysical; if you fail to experience a manifestation but your partner succeeds, or *vice versa*, you both receive reinforcement and the encouragement to press on. Obviously, this partner must bring as much open-minded curiosity and suspension of disbelief to the experiments as you do.)

Upon reaching the meditative state, first try *passive* meditation. This is the most-often-prescribed technique of simply waiting, open-minded, for any psychic or spiritual manifestations that may occur within your consciousness. These may include:

1. *Nothing.* You may discern absolutely nothing paranormal, and feel a bit foolish for "wasting" your time. Be assured that meditation never is a total waste of time; the physical benefits you obtain from the bodily relaxation alone are worth the time. Many individuals go through the ritual every day primarily for the physical rejuvenation.

   Moreover, success in meditation, like most endeavors, improves with practice. All proponents of meditation, of whatever school, advocate practicing daily or twice daily, preferably at the same time or times and in the same environment, for weeks or months if necessary before receiving concrete results. Don't give up!

2. *Impressions.* For lack of a better term, this one serves to describe the most common form of psychic or spiritual input. The "messages" are so undefined and nebulous as to defy concise definition; yet you do experience something that can only be described as impression. To illustrate, when you are engaged in a dream, you sometimes just "know" who is at your side, even though—if you will analyze it carefully—you haven't actually seen or heard this figment in your dream. This sensation of "just

knowing,'' of impressions received that were not visibly or audibly conveyed, is typical of the psychic input most people receive. It's not surprising that if often passes unnoticed, or is dismissed as imagination, and it certainly fails to impress skeptics seeking more explicit and definitive evidence of psychic realities.

Impressions usually require some conscious-mind interpretation; some filling in of the skeleton, so to speak. Of course this invites misinterpretation, too, and contributes to the margin of error inherent in all psychic communications. Most troublesome is the fact that, for most of us, input doesn't come neatly labeled with its source, and it's difficult to distinguish it from imaginative conscious-mind ruminations. With impressions, it is only through continued experience and faith in your higher sources that you can develop confidence in and some validity to your interpretations.

3. *Visualizations*. It's possible that you will find yourself among those who receive psychic input more graphically, in the form of visualizations. You may perceive dreamlike images, which can range from vague and hazy to vividly clear. They may be of individuals, landscapes, panoramas, natural or artificial structures, or simply geometric or random patterns. Even a sensation of infusing light, lacking any detail, can be input.

79

While visualizations sometimes may be literal and explicit revelations, they are more likely to be symbolic. Again, your conscious mind is called into play to interpret the symbolism, and the usual risks of misinterpretation apply. At first, you'll probably have to learn by trial and error how to interpret what you receive, and as you observe your hits and misses, you'll gradually develop confidence in your various symbols.

Despite the contentions of some, there is no universal symbolism code; if your input is symbolic, the significance of the various symbols is unique to you. Another, perceiving the same symbols, may interpret them altogether differently, so it's important that *you* interpret the symbols you perceive, and leave to others interpretation of the symbols they perceive.

Various aspects of the ability to visualize are widely used at the superconscious level for psychic communication. It is this faculty by which authentic psychics perceive auras, crystal-ball visions, glimpses of probable future events, and even dream revelations. The ability to intentionally visualize clearly and in great detail is a vital asset to anyone aggressively pursuing psychic abilities, as well as to anyone engaged in any creative field. It probably can be developed to some extent simply through practice, so if you receive psychic visualizations, by all means invite and develop them.

4. *Audible words*. While it is relatively un-common, some individuals do "hear" their respective Superconsciouses in their minds, perceiving actual words and phrases as clearly as those you hear in dreams. Those who hear spoken messages probably have the advantage of having minimal need for conscious-mind interpre-tation of the communications, although even verbal messages may be couched in parables and punlike plays on words.

If you do hear voices, it will behoove you to be very circumspect in revealing that abil-ity! "Hearing voices" seems to be more in-criminatory in the minds of certain professional practitioners than are "seeing things," "prophesying," "mediumship," etc., even though groundlessly claiming any of these abilities *can* be symptomatic of der-angement.

5. *Physical sensations*. Your Superconscious may impress on you a sensation of warmth or chill, or of floating or gliding, or other more specific physical reactions, although the body may be more receptive to these when it is not in the highly relaxed state sought for meditation. Some individuals, when not in trance, experience strong "gut reactions" to persons or places; actual sensations of visceral discomfort, for in-stance, that warn of potential difficulties or hazards of which they could have no

conscious knowledge. The physical body can be a remarkably sensitive psychic instrument in many ways.

6. *Mental sensations.* Some persons have out-of-the-body experiences, in which they have a sensation of their consciousness leaving the physical body and freely traveling to any destination they think of. This is one manifestation of *astral travel*, although some metaphysicists restrict and qualify this term more narrowly.

Whatever you may choose to call it, some persons in trance (of which the meditative state is one form) do have this experience, often to their considerable alarm, because separation from the body can be unnerving. Apparently this is not just a subjective sensation; some astral travelers are able to return with knowledge they could have obtained only by actual projection of their awareness to a remote location at the given time.[2]

---

[2]Some investigators attribute out-of-body travel to the Spirit's separation from the physical body and subsequent travel. Our concept differs; having confronted Spirits of living persons at locations remote from their physical bodies at times when the mortals were fully conscious and active, we perceive the Spirit as free to travel (or else bilocate) at all times. In out-of-body travel, the subject's *mortal*-level consciousness leaves the body, which then becomes so inert as to resemble suspended animation. Sensitives can perceive this matterless "conscious body" as it separates from and rejoins the inert physical body, which possesses no aura while the consciousness is absent. This is *not* the Spirit, which is separately discernible to the sensitive; we sometimes think of this as the "soul," an aspect which survives physical death and is observed to subsequently merge with its Spirit.

While the likelihood is small, if you should happen to experience out-of-body or astral travel, it probably will be initially very brief. The natural alarm at perceiving your body apart from "you" is likely to startle you out of trance, snapping "you" instantly and a bit unceremoniously back into your body. As you progress with meditation and psychic research, you may find astral travel less unnerving and engage in it more readily. It is important to realize that your physical body is totally inert and barely idling while "you" are out of it, so you should undertake astral travel only when you can lie on a bed or floor and are quite certain that your body will be undisturbed and secure in the interim.

If you or your partner experience any of these manifestations as a result of one or several periods of meditation, you may be tempted to dismiss them as mere imagination (or suggestibility, from having read of them here). Bear in mind, though, that imagination is actually an exercise of your creative faculties, and your Superconscious is your highest creative aspect, so that what seems imaginary may be valid input. Suspend judgment, continue to experiment, and seek ways to confirm the validity of your results. If you are actually communicating with your Superconscious, you eventually will be able to confirm its validity to your satisfaction, even though it may be to no one else's.

Thus far, we've discussed only passive meditation, in which you simply wait for something to happen. There is a more aggressive form of alpha-level exercise taught in assorted guises by the various self-realization schools of thought, for such goals as reprogramming of personality, overcoming limitations and hang-ups, and generally reshaping one's personal reality. Using essentially the same physical and mental relaxation countdown techniques, these exercises require you to enter the meditative trance state with a specific objective, question, or goal, rather than simply waiting passively for something to "drop in." I call this approach *directed* meditation, and it may bring more definitive results than the passive method. One student of metaphysics, seeking evidence of the existence of his Superconscious through directed meditation asking if there was "anyone there," was startled when he visualized an imposing, Mr. Clean-like figure and perceived a commanding, imperious "I AM!" It certainly worked for him.

If you'd like to try directed meditation, an interesting experiment is to invite your Superconscious to give you its name. You will recall from Chapter 1 that it is convenient to treat the distinct personality of your Spirit virtually as another individual, having a separate name by which to address it. We find that most Superconsciouses have distinct preferences as to the name by which they like to be addressed, and they will reveal their preferences to those who are receptive to their communications. Therefore, a valid question to use as the focus of your first directed meditation, as you attempt to establish contact with your higher self, is: "What shall I call you?" You may get an answer!

The answer probably won't come thundering into your mind like the voice of God, and it probably won't appear as a name tag in your mind's eye (although either manifestation certainly is possible). But if you go into the meditative state with this question foremost, be alert to the very first name that enters your mind. You may tend to discount a name's popping vaguely into your head as the natural toying of your conscious mind with possible names, but in fact it's equally likely that the name was planted there by your Superconscious. Unless other names later come to mind with much stronger emphasis or insistence, that very first one probably is a name your SC will be comfortable with and responsive to. And should it not be, that fact will become evident in some fashion or other in your subsequent attempts at communication.

An interesting experiment is to invite your Superconscious to speak aloud through your physical vocal chords. To try this, have your partner first conduct you through the relaxation countdown into the trance state; then, by prearrangement, have him or her respectfully ask your Superconscious to speak through you. If it chooses not to, you will remain silent, but if it does choose to cooperate, you may experience any of several reactions:

1. You feel a strong desire to say hello. *Don't resist it*; say whatever you feel the urge to, because that desire to speak does not originate in your conscious mind, even

85

though you'll think it does. You will seem to be consciously groping for words and expressions, because your Superconscious is working through your conscious mind and vocabulary to put into words the impressions it wants to convey. While others who know you well will detect some differences in your phrasing and inflections during the manifestation of your Superconscious, you will find it difficult to accept it for what it claims to be. With patience and time, you may hear yourself giving information of which you have no conscious knowledge (but which later proves to be accurate), or expressing an opinion with which you strongly disagree, and you'll be more or less forced to accept this higher personality of your Spirit.

2. You may perceive words "forming themselves" in your mind a split second before you hear your lips speak them, all without your volition. This will surprise you, but it will leave little doubt that these words are coming from something other than your conscious mind. They are, of course; they're from your Superconscious.

3. You may go so deeply into trance that you are conscious of nothing, and be quite surprised when your partner calls you back to awareness and recounts what "you" said. If you recorded the session on tape, you'll be able to hear for yourself exactly what

was said via your voice while your conscious awareness was out to lunch. If you can't accept that *this* communication originated elsewhere then your conscious mind, your skepticism verges on hopeless!

Parenthetically, if this sounds much like your concept of deep-trance hypnosis, that's because it involves essentially the same state(s) of mind(s), except that some aspect of *you* is in control, rather than the hypnotist. Hypnotic techniques conventionally are explained in terms of extracting information from the subject's "subconscious," but in truth, it is the Superconscious that responds to the competent hypnotist.

If it turns out that your Superconscious is vocal, you will find it to have a personality that is different and distinct from yours, and it will be confusing and inappropriate for your partner in these experiments to call it by your name. This is why most SCs will suggest a different name by which to address them. All you or your partner need do is ask, and you probably will be given a name. The name it chooses may be a common, contemporary one, an old-fashioned one, or a biblical or exotic one. Whatever, it will have some particular significance to your Superconscious at this time, although it may give you a different one after you get better acquainted.

It is important to prepare you for the possibility of the Superconscious of a male mortal choosing a feminine name, and *vice versa*. It can be a little unsettling for a man to learn that his Superconscious chooses Marilyn, or for a woman's to choose Max. Be assured here that *the gender of the Superconscious's name casts no reflection on the sexuality of the mortal.* We understand the Spirits to be androgynous; the physical differences, responsibilities, and pleasures of sex exist only in the mortal universe (one of the experiences for which Spirits incarnate). The Superconscious's choice of names is not indicative of gender at the spiritual level, although it may be indicative of attitude; it's quite possible for a Spirit to express male chauvinist views. Notice, though, that while I have referred to the Superconscious (and Spirit) as ''it,'' once given a name for yours, you will find it linguistically convenient to refer to it as ''him'' or ''her,'' as the case may be.

Your Superconscious may initially give a name of the same gender as yours simply to ease your adjustment in accepting its existence and manifested presence, all the while preferring one of opposite gender. It then is likely that after you become fully comfortable with your higher self's presence and are not threatened by implications of gender, your SC will request you to switch to another name for it. This seems to occur with some frequency among women, who may first be given a feminine SC name but may later be asked to switch to a masculine one. In my experience, it is rare—but not unheard of— for a man to be given a feminine SC name.

Whatever it may wish to be called, your Superconscious can be most helpful to the purpose of this book if it will manifest vocally through you. The fundamental objective behind these pages is to declare and emphasize the fact that each human has his own higher consciousness and purpose; that he has a direct source for acquiring knowledge of other levels of reality; that he has *within himself* a God-consciousness that can be cultivated to benefit himself and his society. If you can personally experience convincing manifestations of your Superconscious—and vocal ones are highly persuasive—it will greatly enhance the credibility of this book in your eyes, and provide you an alternate, personal authority through which you can test, and confirm or refute, the doctrines presented here. A vocal Superconscious can transform these statements from mere words on paper to a deep, personal involvement in new realities.

And what can you expect from a communicative Superconscious? Spiritual, God-oriented messages? Will it remonstrate with you for your mortal shortcomings and indiscretions? Will it bolster your resolve in the face of temptation? Perhaps, and hopefully so, but much Superconscious input is more mundane and goal-oriented than inspirational. And therein lies another factor in the human proclivity for conflict: *there is little unanimity of direction among the Spirits*. They are not clones; each was given free will at its creation, so that it might become an individual—and individualism resists concerted effort.

You can see the effect of personal free will at work in your own life: your parents tried to instill in you those dogmas, values, and morals in which they believed and which they felt are essential to your lifelong well-being and to society's health. During your early years, you were forced to abide by their ideology; your free will was subjugated by overriding parental authority. As you grew older and were able to assert your free will, you abandoned or modified some of that parentally programmed ideology according to your own perceptions, experiences, and reasoning, so that you became more individual and less a carbon copy of your parents.

While your childhood programming occurred piecemeal over several years and was never so total as the instantaneous "charging" of the Spirits with the God-intellect, the principle of free will's shaping of the individual applies similarly to them. So not all Spirits now think and act like God. In fact we are told that some, like some mortals you know, have rebelled and totally rejected the values with which they once were infused. In other words, Spirits, like mortals, range in their individual ideologies through the entire spectrum from "good" to "bad." It is important to note, however, that just as you never will forget the ideology instilled by your parents (and you may reembrace some of its valid tenets as your judgment matures), the Spirits have not lost the God-aspect instilled at their creation. Even the most derelict of them still carries an embedded "corpuscle of God." *It is this element of divinity in each Spirit human—no matter how obscure and latent it may be—that makes man sacrosanct.* In our Western culture, we hold human life to be sacred not because man became the most remarkable of the animals through some series of presumed evolutionary accidents, but because he is immutably endowed with an aspect of God.

Then this is the important ingredient you look for in the manifestations of your Superconscious: evidence of the God-aspect; a sense of higher purpose. Your SC may be a source of much information about what we classify as paranormal phenomena, and it may respond to the more frivolous questions prompted by your curiosity, but you should also expect guidance for living an exemplary mortal life. We understand that many—perhaps most—incarnate Spirits are seeking at this point in the universe's evolution to incorporate their learning experiences into ideologies that will be compatible, in their ultimate resolution, with God's.

Because the ideologies your conscious mind constructs in this mortal experience become part of the total ideology of your Spirit—of *you*—it is to your mortal and Spiritual advantage to attune your conscious mind to your superconscious one. By inviting communication from your higher mind, by engaging in dialogue with it, you will be better able to guide your conscious thoughts and attitudes into harmony with your higher self. This, I contend, is the *real* meaning of the *attunement* sought by religious seekers.

Working toward this attunement may require a generous measure of faith. Goals set at the superconscious level may not be comprehensible, or even apparent, at the conscious-mind level, and your Superconscious sometimes may appear to be nudging you in seemingly strange directions. Unless you perceive these directions to be inimical to your fellow man, give them a try; your SC can anticipate cause-and-effect equations farther than can your mortal powers of reason. Invest a little faith and see what happens.

The idea of following the lead of your Superconscious—of working toward attunement—may seem to threaten your conscious-level free will. But your free will always works to advance your conscious-mind goals; when those are aligned with the goals of your Superconscious, there's no conflict.

Adopting lofty values as your own—that is, attuning yourself to them—eliminates the free-will conflict that otherwise results from conforming to externally imposed constraints. When it's *your* ideal, your free will is directed toward its achievement.

If you can develop *faith* in the worthiness of your Superconscious's objectives, you'll be on the road to attunement. Mary Baker Eddy said, ''To live so as to keep human consciousness in constant relation with the divine, the spiritual, and the eternal, is to individualize infinite power.''[3] This is not a promise of personal or material power on the mortal level, but rather an affirmation of the God-given power of spiritual insight to reach exalted goals when your Spirit has its several aspects attuned in a unified whole. In other words, when you've got it all together. So, try attunement. Right now. Or at the first convenient time you can set aside, before you go on to the next chapter. You may be surprised!

---

[3]Mary Baker Eddy, *The First Church of Christ, Scientist, and Miscellany.*

Chapter 7

SPIRITS AT LARGE

We will draw the curtain and show you the picture.

—Shakespeare
Twelfth Night

From here on, the rule is: don't integrate any concept into your personal belief structure that your Superconscious disagrees with. Including those anywhere in this book. The only condition on this rule is to be sure it's your *Super*conscious—not the rational side of your conscious mind—that is doing the disagreeing.

By bringing your SC into your deliberations, you are calling upon an aspect of you that has countless eons of experience, because you—the Spirit you—have existed for millions of years. You were created in that cosmic God-thought that abruptly populated the entire universe with formless, sentient beings, and the immortal part of you has been a thinking, seeking individual ever since. Just as your conscious-level curiosity (and perhaps the guidance of your Superconscious) has led you to this book for whatever value you may glean, so has your Spirit (in common with all others) sought to experience and to learn as much as possible of every level of existence.

You might suppose that a few million years would be enough to experience everything several times over and become utterly bored, especially when you can transcend the limitations of physical space and time, but this may reflect only our mortal ignorance of the magnitude of creation. After all, just that part of the physical universe that we can perceive from earth is mind-boggling. In our own Milky Way galaxy, there are an estimated three hundred billion stars, while within view of our most powerful optical telescopes, which can reach out a few billion light-years,[1] are approximately one hundred million galaxies, with perhaps as many as one billion galaxies believed to be in the universe. This implies about three hundred million trillion stars—a totally incomprehensible number. How long would it take you to "experience" every one of these stars if you allowed just *one second* for each, and required no travel time to refocus your

[1] One light-year is the distance light will travel in space in one year; about five trillion, eight hundred seventy billion miles. At a nominal ninety-three million miles, our sun is about eight light-*minutes* away. (References here to the quantity one billion refer to the American usage of the term as one thousand million; a trillion is a million million.)

94

awareness from one star to the next? Simple arithmetic gives the answer: more than ten *trillion* years! Since we believe the current version of the material universe is only a few billion years old, it's evident that no single entity has explored it all. This really isn't surprising; after the first hundred million or so, stars must begin to look alike, anyway.

Backing off and taking a more cosmic view, though, would give you another fascinating panorama. The universe is a dynamic environment whose parts are in a perpetual state of creation, maturation, and demise, but our mortal time constraints allow us only a still-frame snapshot of this evolution. How magnificent must be the sight of a spiral galaxy as it reveals the maelstrom of creation, the kaleidoscopic coalescence of consolidation, and the scintillating throes of extinction, all over the course of a few billion years. Even to a consciousness jaded by countless and endless celestial extravaganzas, this must be a compelling sight!

Beyond the fascination of matter in metamorphosis, though, is an element of far greater interest to your living Spirit: physical life. From the simplest, single-cell structure to the most incredibly complex, physical life forms are of particular spiritual interest, for they share with your Spirit the God-given facilities of volition and creation. It is in the successive, generation-by-generation procreations and permutations of physical life forms that your Spirit may express its own creative powers—manipulating a genetic molecule here or there and observing the result. We understand that this directed evolution of physical life on earth has occupied some Spirits for millions of years, culminating in the biped mammal deemed suitable for the Spirits to inhabit in their quest for direct physical experience. You may have had an influence in the design of your own body!

Similar experiments evidently have taken place on other worlds, as well—perhaps with your participation. While our scientists are still speculating about the mere existence of planets around other stars, and the possibility of life on some of them, we are told that there are indeed intelligent, God-fearing, mortal beings on other worlds somewhere in the universe.[2] Because they are inhabited by Spirits, just as you and I are, these other-world beings are *human* in the broadest sense of the word. Science has yet to realize—or even contemplate—that whenever we *do* meet intelligent, creative beings from some other world, we will be meeting fellow humans! Their physical differences may be great, but they will be spiritual brothers. We may fervently hope *they* recognize the brotherhood, since many of us may not.

In addition to its attention to the physical universe, your Spirit also occupies itself with matters—probably many more than we can ever comprehend from our mortal viewpoint—in the nonphysical realm. We can deduce a few of these concerns, though, if we attribute those very same characteristics to the superconscious mind that we

---

[2] With three hundred million trillion stars, the chances of planets—even planets supportive of physical life as we know it—seem pretty good.

know are properties of the conscious mind. There is no great risk of error in this assumption, since we understand the conscious mind to be simply a segment of the Superconscious that is isolated to some degree. Therefore our thought processes and reactions on the conscious level rely on the same basic structures of logic, reason, and emotion as do those on the superconscious level, and we need not speculate about some mysterious, unfathomable "spiritual" rationale that is beyond mortal understanding. The differences between the levels of intellect are in knowledge, experience, and scope of vision, not in the mechanics of thought.

Given a society of billions of beings, each with free will and many millennia of individual experiences shaping their unique personalities, some structure of social order is an obvious necessity. Anarchy is as unworkable at the Spirits' level as at the mortals', and there long has been a directing spiritual hierarchy to forestall the chaos that otherwise would prevail. Even though all Spirits initially were created with equal status, just below the First-Born, the diversity of their subsequently emerging personalities marked some as leaders and others as followers—with some, as we shall see, who conform to neither pattern. So there are administrators and workers and shirkers, teachers and students, thinkers and activists, enthusiasts and the apathetic; the whole gamut of characteristics and interests found in any society of free-willed individuals, albeit that they are expressed principally on nonmaterial levels.

These acitivities and interests are among the experiences that have kept the Spirits occupied for what we perceive as millions of years. So while you—the Spirit you—may have done your share of star-gazing, you also have engaged in prolonged social interaction on a universal scale, paralleling what the conscious aspect of you is now doing on the physical level. At every level, the names of the game are "experience" and "learning," which are expected to lead you to intellectual and spiritual growth.

As in any society, there are those in the spiritual realm who rebel at the social structure. Free will begets personality, personality begets ego, and ego tends to seek self-aggrandizement. We are told of a Spirit who early occupied an exalted position in the established hierarchy and whose charismatic personality attracted legions of adherents whose loyalty was to that individual, rather than to his office. He allowed his supplicants to inflate his ego to the point where he was emboldened to challenge the First-Born for rulership of the entire spiritual domain. His audacity exceeded his power, however, for God is not disposed to subrogation of His First-Born by any other, and the rebellious Spirit was ejected from the hierarchy.

And so it is today, we are told, that we have in the spiritual realm a dichotomy of purpose. The fallen angel, Lucifer—whose name means "Bearer of Light," reflecting on his former position—and many of his adherents still captivated by his charisma and promises, are in conflict with the established hierarchy and the many Spirits committed to it. Caught in the crossfire of this dichotomy is a great body of Spirits not presently committed to either side who are fair game for the blandishments and entreaties of both. A major battleground for this conflict is on the mortal level, and you may have a role, to some degree, in this classic confrontation between practitioners of good and perpetrators of evil.

There is a growing school of thought which contends that "good" and "evil" exist only in the conscious perceptions of man and are arbitrarily and pragmatically defined by him; however, we understand from our discussion in Chapter 5 that *if* there is a sentient, volitional God, it is axiomatic that there are absolutes: that which advances the plan of God is good; that which impedes it is wrong; and that which willfully opposes it is evil.

Notice the distinction here between *wrong* and *evil.* The word evil carries the connotation of *intentional* wrong. Therefore you can inadvertently commit an offense—a wrong—through ignorance, oversight, or failure to anticipate the consequences, without being evil, but *to intentionally perform an act that you perceive to be wrong* is *evil.*[3] This is our definition of *sin,* and we are given to under-

---

[3]This refutes those who contend that physical man is born innately evil because of his precivilized, inherent animal ancestry and his capacity to display animal behavior. Having no understanding of right and wrong, an animal cannot be evil, so the human animal is *not* born innately evil; only ignorant. As an individual gains knowledge of right and wrong, his continuing failure to transcend animalistic behavior may manifest as evil, but that evil comes from his *mind,* not his innocent physical nature. Even our body of law recognizes this; a person provably unable to discern right from wrong is not held criminally accountable for his offenses against humanity. God's law similarly distinguishes between evil and ignorance.

stand there truly are spiritual entities dedicated to sin—to willfully opposing God's plan. It would be comforting to embrace the position of the many metaphysical guides and teachers who deny the existence of a perniciously oriented intellect in the universe, but our Spirit authorities unanimously and emphatically proclaim the existence of Lucifer and his multitude of minions. There *is* an evil influence abroad in the spiritual realm and, insofar as Lucifer's incarnate supporters are able to manifest through their mortals, it is abroad in our physical world, too.

From this oversimplified view, one could get the idea that the Spirits have done little for millions of years but knock around the universe, indulge in creation as a hobby, and choose sides in an ideological dispute. Entering the physical plane on earth for a few decades—a mere eye-blink, relative to eons of Spirit existence—seems almost anticlimactic in comparison. And evidently the cycle of incarnation *is* too brief to accomplish all that most Spirits are expected to learn from the mortal experience; our sources are unanimous in confirming that ongoing repetition of the physical cycle is practiced by most Spirits. This repetition is embodied in the concept known to most of us as *reincarnation*. While it is not accepted today in conventional Judeo-Christian dogma, the fact is that, worldwide, more people believe in reincarnation than do not, and it seems a worthy topic to which to devote the next chapter.

Chapter 8

"PLAY IT AGAIN, SAM"

How many ages hence
Shall this our lofty scene
be acted o'er
In states unborn and accents
yet unknown!

—Shakespeare
Julius Caesar

I never believed in reincarnation. I've believed all my thinking life in a spiritual aspect of man that survives mortal death; I've been comfortable with the concept of a Supreme Intellect; I have expected to reunite in some exalted realm with the personalities of loved ones; but I've had no room for a belief in having lived previous mortal lives.

I certainly can't give a rational reason for my aversion. Why should I find this particular concept, among a large number of engaging concepts equally

101

preposterous at face value, so difficult for me to even investigate? Maybe it poses some threat at an emotional level? Does the prospect of having lived before somehow destroy the uniqueness of my present life? Does it suggest that what I am today is not entirely a product of whatever talents and limitations, ambitions and lethargies, strengths and foibles that I brought to this lifetime? In ways that I can't express, the concept of reincarnation somehow threatened my sense of individuality, my sense of "me-ness."

I certainly read about reincarnation; about those who, like Bridey Murphy, seemed to recall other lives and details of other times and places that proved historically accurate. Some of the writings on the subject are very scholarly and conservative, convincingly substantiating the apparent fact that some subjects do "recall" accurate information. Being committed to disbelief in this particular concept, I was able to structure an alternate explanation for such "recall" that I found more satisfactory.[1]

But the study of metaphysics is conducive to changing one's beliefs about many facets of personal reality, and my resistance to reincarnation finally crumbled under the onslaught of our most respected higher sources. They unanimously assert

---

[1]That alternate explanation may still be viable. If indeed there is some static repository in which are stored every detail of every entity's life, then it seems no more improbable that a person in trance might be able to "read" from these records than that he might be able to "remember" lives that predate his present physical existence. In my antireincarnation days, this sort of clairvoyance seemed much more acceptable than the concept of previous physical lives.

that reincarnation does exist. In fact, I don't know offhand of any Spirit source that denies the fact of reincarnation, although some differ markedly in their descriptions of the ways in which it manifests. Perhaps reincarnation is the only metaphysical concept that is universally proclaimed by all allegedly higher sources.

If it is true that reincarnation is the rule of the universe, it seems unfortunate that modern Judeo-Christian dogma doesn't recognize it; that in fact the very concept is anathema to the main-line denominations. Some metaphysicists claim that reincarnation was taken for granted by the early Christians, but that because of pressure by Justinian, the Fifth Ecumenical Council at Constantinople in 553, undertook to excise from the Bible all references to it. Among our own sources, one says, "The originals of many of the Bible's books were loaded with references [to reincarnation], but the early church leaders found it very difficult to control their flocks without the hellfire-and-brimstone approach that [the concept of] one life and one life only lends itself to, so the early references were deleted."

This allegation is one wherein I must defer to research by the various experts in Bible history and early religions. It does seem, though, that— if they once were there—possibly some references to reincarnation escaped the eagle eye of the censor. And in fact those who assert that reincarnation was accepted, or at least recognized in concept, by early Christians have fastened on a

103

few New Testament passages that seem to suggest exactly that.

Speaking to the disciples in Matthew 17, Jesus said, ". . . But I say to you that Elijah has already come, and they knew him not, but have done to him whatever they wanted." Then, Matthew tells us, the disciples understood that he spoke of John the Baptist. This is confirmed earlier in Matthew (11:14–15), when Jesus said about John the Baptist, "And if you wish to accept it, that he is Elijah who was to come. He who has ears to hear, let him hear."

It's interesting that John the Baptist denied being Elijah. This suggests that he, like most modern-day humans, had no conscious recollection of previous lives and, since Elijah was a highly exalted figure of Jewish history, humble modesty surely prevented John from seriously considering even the possibility.

Some may argue that this is a special case since, according to the biblical account, Elijah was spared mortal death by being taken away in a whirlwind, and it was promised that he would return (Malachi 4:5). Yet few, I can safely venture, would suggest that Elijah returned to be John the Baptist in the same fleshly body in which he left as Elijah. Further, John's birth and growth to adulthood are known to have occurred within the context of his mortal life; evidently there was no surreptitious exchanging of bodies involved.

It seems the Bible can be quoted and interpreted to prove almost any viewpoint, so these passages suggesting an acceptance of reincarnation in

Christ's time are hardly compelling by themselves. They do, however, lend some support to the consistent and insistent affirmation of reincarnation's reality by our Spirit sources, adding to whatever other evidence we can muster.

If we are to give it serious consideration, then we must define reincarnation more explicitly than I have yet done. Those to whom reincarnation is just a word often suppose it to include physical lifetimes as animals, which is more correctly called *transmigration*. No doubt this belief arises from the fact that one of the major Hindu religions teaches that one's soul (Spirit?) incarnates at various times into certain species of animals along the way to spiritual evolution and enlightenment, and this is why the cow, for instance, is sacred in India and revered amongst the starving masses rather than eaten. This concept is *not* accepted within the framework of reincarnation as discussed here, even though some dictionaries erroneously list transmigration as a synonym for reincarnation.

Another common misconception about reincarnation is that one exists in all lives as the same mortal; that one who is John Jones in his present life was the same individual, even though he may have had a different name and lived elsewhere in the world, in all previous lifetimes; that he probably looked as he does this time and had the same personality and talents. This is totally counter to reincarnation as it is perceived by students of metaphysics. Only the Spirit is common to all lifetimes; the mortals in which that Spirit resides down through its succession of lifetimes ordinarily are vastly different from one another, being sometimes male, sometimes female; sometimes of one race and sometimes another. Personalities and talents are equally as varied; one objective of successive incarnations is to experience the gamut of human endeavors and conditions, which certainly rules out mere clones of the same mortal. At the conscious level, each of these incarnations is a unique individual (establishing this uniqueness is one reason for isolation of the conscious mind from the superconscious one, which retains memories of all its previous incarnations). The only common element is the Spirit, the superconscious mind of which assimilates all the experiences and lessons of the several mortal extensions it has fostered.[2]

While most metaphysicists accept reincarnation, not all agree that the various mortal experiences of a given individual are lived in successive intervals. Seth, the entity who dictated metaphysical essays to the late Jane Roberts, alludes to the concept of a given Spirit's *simultaneously* experiencing multiple lifetimes, which only appear from this physical level to be occurring in different time periods. In fact, carried far enough, his concept allows a certain overlap *within our physical time frame* of

---

[2] It is interesting to speculate on the effect that acceptance of reincarnation would have on bigots of various stripes: if you genuinely believed that the "real you" had previously existed as someone you had always thought to be inferior to yourself—*or if you understood that you might do so in the future*—it certainly would require revising your old values! Perhaps this is one factor in the reluctance of so many to even examine the concept of reincarnation.

mortal lives, so that the mortal "you" conceivably could encounter another living mortal who shares your Spirit in the present.

This argument develops from the universally accepted idea that time and space are indeterminant in the nonphysical realms; that only in physical reality can we define those quantities. One can do some neat tricks with equations and semantics to prove that time, as we understand it, can't even be *defined* without including terms of physical mass (or energy, which is another form of mass) and its movement in physical space, and it may be that past, present, and future do not flow linearly for perceivers on nonphysical levels. Perhaps this is the tack Seth is taking in his contention that, from the astral point of view, lifetimes can occur "simultaneously."

But if all were indeed simultaneous, then all would be instantaneous; there could be no beginning and no end, and eternity would be less than an instant! This is contradictory, or it's beyond mortal comprehension; either way, we prefer the simpler concept: there is a sequential flow of events even in the nonphysical realms, so that each mortal-life experience occupies a unique position in a Spirit's sequence of reincarnations. Within this concept, there must be duration and passage of time on the other levels, although it may not be definable in convenient and consistent units. Perhaps it's something like *subjective* time, which varies according to the activity you're engaged in. A clock hour spent at something you greatly enjoy seems frustratingly short, while another clock hour spent at an extremely distasteful task seems interminable. In other words, subjective time—your perception of the rate at which the past recedes and the future approaches—can't be uniformly and rigidly defined; nevertheless, events subjectively do have duration and they do occur in sequence. This analogy may be as close as we can come on this level to an understanding of time as it functions in the non-physical realms.

Whatever may be true of absolute time, our sources reject any simultaneity of mortal existences. A major objective of the physical experience is to learn; if there were no flow of time toward a future, there would be no duration in which to compile individual experiences, draw inferences from them, and apply the lessons learned to subsequent activities. Confusing the issue with esoteric arguments about the nonexistence of time on other levels and a simultaneity of mortal lives obscures any understanding of reincarnation, which is difficult enough to grasp at best. So we're comfortable in our understanding that Spirits, like we mortals, perceive events to flow in cause-and-effect sequences, even if the *durations* of those sequences can't be neatly bundled in seconds, minutes, hours, or years. In our book, a Spirit lives but one mortal existence at a time.

So far, we've established as our foundation of reincarnation that we do not return to each life as a clone of the mortal we were in the previous life; that we do not incarnate in the lesser animals in some form of spiritual evolution, and that we do not share our respective Spirits with other mortals existing in the same physical era. These are the things, as we understand it, that reincarnation is *not*. We have yet to attack the question of what it *is*.

Or perhaps *why* it is. The "what" is simple enough: many Spirits either choose to or are directed to incarnate in mortal form not once, but some number of times as ages pass. Each time, the mortal form encounters unique experiences as it moves from conception to physical death; experiences that are retained in the immortal memory of the Spirit and become a part of its ever-evolving individuality. Along the way, there also are lessons to be learned—but that's for another chapter. Here we're interested in the commitment to experience. And we're free to speculate as widely as we choose.

It seems logically acceptable to hypothesize that nothing more mysterious than curiosity (at some level) underlies this drive for broad experience, just as curiosity is a prime motivator among many research scientists in their quest for new knowledge. Curiosity seems to be an inherent characteristic of intellect and, if there is a universal Supreme Intellect—the mind of God or the Godhead—it must have a supreme curiosity. Then it would follow that the Spirits, being autonomous projections of God, would share that curiosity in due proportion and would actively seek to indulge it. This may in itself be sufficient to explain their reincarnation for several varied lifetimes in the physical plane.

We can carry our speculation a step farther, though. We understand that the goal of most Spirits is to reunite—to merge—with the Godhead;[3] evidently they were charged at their creation to go forth and experience all the universe and then return to share that experience. Even though God stereotypically is considered omniscient, it may be more realistic to recognize that even the most fantastic intellect finds vicarious experience inferior to actuality. And it may be equally realistic to suppose that even God, as a singular entity, would find it difficult to directly undergo every possible experience in an indescribably vast physical universe. With these assumptions, we can understand how a Supreme Intellect might, just to indulge its supreme curiosity, spawn untold billions of sporelike Spirits and charge each to accumulate experiences and return to share them with their Creator.

To better grasp how sharing of the diverse experiences would function at this uppermost level, liken the early Godhead to a pristine lake entirely devoid of foreign matter. The sun, shining on this lake, evaporates pure water from its surface and the atmosphere causes it to form in a cloud composed of countless individual vapor droplets. Each droplet is a ''corpuscle'' of the parent lake, endowed with the same proportions of hydrogen and oxygen and constrained by the same intera-

---

[3] The concept of a Godhead having plurality, instead of singularity, is suggested on the first page of the Bible, Genesis 1:1. Being neither Bible scholar nor ancient-language authority, I must accept the assertion of others that the Hebrew word translated in Genesis 1:1 as ''God'' is *Elohim*, which is said to carry the connotation of plurality; a God(head) comprised of more than one person or individuality.

tomic energy patterns, as are to be found in that lake. However, the droplet is already becoming individualized through exposure to the gases and particulate matter in the atmosphere. The surrounding vapor drops are undergoing virtually identical experiences and are more or less clones of one another. Were this cloud then to rain upon the lake, that body would assume the "experiences" of the individual drops as they merged with it. And the drops would lose their individuality, but their "experiences" ultimately would diffuse throughout the entire lake to the benefit of the whole.

This singular "incarnation," however, would not greatly broaden the "experience" level of the lake, since nearly all returning drops underwent essentially similar, limited experiences. In fact, however, most of the vapor droplets evaporated from the lake and formed in clouds will not fall immediately back into the lake, but will move overland and fall on the ground. Perhaps some drops will collect in surface puddles, where they "experience" soil, grass, insects, microbes, and animals. Others may soak through the soil all the way to the subterranean water table and emerge miles away in a spring, carrying with them the "experiences" of subsoil organisms, limestone and sand strata, and various minerals. Still other drops may be swallowed by thirsting animals and undergo many transformations and organic "experiences" along the way.

A given drop may be evaporated and renewed as

rain many times,[4] analogous to physical dying and reincarnating. The intervals between "lives" correspond to the interludes spent in the clouds; the mortal incarnations are experienced upon falling back to earth as rain. Ultimately, in one year or a hundred thousand, that drop will again fall into the parent lake, bringing with it all its accumulated "experiences." In the process of merging, the returning drop loses its individuality and becomes simply a part of the sea, thereafter indistinguishable from all the other drops that collectively make up the lake.

The "experiences" of the returning drops diffuse among all the other drops present, and the lake becomes a homogeneous amalgam of vast "knowledge." No longer is it the pristine reservoir of innocence it was; it now is the repository of seemingly infinite knowledge. Yet there is a paradox: the entire body of experiences behind that knowledge—experiences that required billions of individual drops to accumulate—now are contained in, and can be inferred from, any single drop of water taken from the lake. Our oceans are exemplary of this phenomenon; traces or evidence of practically every chemical element and compound naturally occurring on earth can be found in any sample of ocean water, in proportions determined

---

[4]To maintain the analogy, we have to neglect the fact that water, when evaporated, loses the minerals and other materials dissolved in it. For our purposes here, assume that a given drop retains all its "experiences" through its entire series of "incarnations." Further, we have to endow the lowly raindrop with a fictional complexity that allows it to carry these "experiences" into a new life without being consciously "aware" of them in that life!

by their abundance and the history of earth's weathering and erosion. In latter years, unnatural, manmade compounds have found their way to the seas, adding to the history—the evidential knowledge—that can be discerned in a single drop of ocean water.

If in fact God has charged the Spirits to experience as much of the universe as possible and then to merge with the Godhead, it follows from our analogy that the collective body of knowledge accruing from unknown billions of Spirits acting through eons of time would be vast beyond mortal comprehension. If God isn't as omniscient now as He's alleged to be, just wait! With time and experience, omniscience will come. And since knowledge is power, omnipotence surely must come with it.

Again, the question arises: why this compulsion for unlimited knowledge? Is it adequately explained by nothing more than the natural curiosity of an exalted Intellect? Or is there some purpose—some application—to be made of it?

It's outrageously presumptuous to second-guess God, I'm sure. But I do presume that the power of curiosity can be obsessive to an entity of pure intellect. According to the Big Bang theory of the origin of the universe, there exists a possibility that the entire domain will rebound from its present outward expansion and ultimately collapse upon itself in one great cataclysm of gravitational paroxysm. If this is correct, there is a finite time remaining for the Godhead to acquire the absolute totality of experiences possible in this physical reality before it ceases to exist in its present form.

I venture to suggest that the knowledge obtained from all possible experiences in this physical reality will be vital to improving the design of the next one. When the physical universe collapses into a ball of inconceivable energy and again explodes with a "big bang," the new universe may be unrecognizable in terms of our present concepts. The physical laws of mass, velocity, gravity, and electromagnetism may be entirely different; life forms may be metabolically inscrutable, and even darkness and light may not exist as we know them. But whatever differences this new model may have, if they are inspired by the knowledge the Creator acquired from experiences in the present one, it will represent a forward step in the evolution of universes and in the physical life forms that come to inhabit them. And, should the Godhead again separate from itself a host of Spirits, each of them— like each drop of lake water in our analogy—will possess all the knowledge accrued by the Godhead in the previous incarnation of the universe, giving to each a vastly superior foundation from which to perform its new roles.

Fanciful speculation, this—but it *could* explain the importance that seems to attach to the physical experience of the individual Spirit. If the prime intent of the Creator is to recycle physical reality in progressive steps toward perfection, it follows that it is the Spirits' experiences as physical entities that are most pertinent to the cause. Thus it would follow that to undergo a number of lifetimes, under greatly differing circumstances, may be the objective of many Spirits.

Whether this be true or not, we do understand that there are other, more personal, reasons for Spirits to reincarnate numerous times; among them being the learning of lessons. This aspect of reincarnation is inextricably intertwined with the subject of the next chapter and will be elaborated on there.

In the meantime, you may harbor some curiosity about any former lives you—the higher you—may have experienced. If you're like most, you have no conscious memories of having lived previously, although many persons feel vaguely familiar with some occupations or seem drawn to certain countries or geographical locations without knowing why. On the other hand, it's not at all rare for a person to catch glimpses or receive impressions of existing in some other circumstances and surroundings when they seek, in meditation, to do so. So, if you do have some curiosity about possible past lives, do what is by now the obvious: using the exercise in Chapter 14 or your own method, go into the meditative state and ask to be shown scenes from a past life.

Let me qualify that suggestion for your first effort: life generally was more oppressive and hazardous in generations past, and it is possible to reexperience something quite unpleasant or disturbing while in trance, so be sure to ask your higher self this time to allow you to perceive only pleasant interludes from one of your more carefree lives. Should you later become interested in seriously researching your past reincarnations, you can mentally prepare yourself to cope with the more traumatic incidents you may be shown.[5]

How do past-life scenes manifest themselves? The answers are as varied as the people seeking them. Sometimes only vague impressions of sights, or sounds, or smells, or sensations. Perhaps a fleeting image of a landscape, an edifice, a gathering of persons, or a sky. Perhaps an entire sequence, like a dream, flowing from beginning to the end of an entire episode. Perhaps with others whom you somehow recognize from this lifetime, even though they have a different appearance and different relationship to you. And of course you may receive absolutely nothing. Nobody promised you total success!

If you do receive some sort of impression, how do you tell it from raw imagination? You don't. Not at first, anyway. Going into an altered state and receiving images or impressions proves nothing about past lives, and you should not accept it as proof. However, if you pursue research and obtain additional details that tend to flesh out your early impressions, and if other psychics proffer corroborating perceptions about some of the past-

---

[5] Hypnotists have a technique to permit their subjects to relive traumatic incidents during hypnotic recall without reexperiencing the emotional trauma, which *can* be as disturbing as the initial incident. They advise the hypnotized subject that he will be able to observe himself from a third-person viewpoint and thereby remain detached from the trauma. This resembles seeing one's self as though from out of the body. A similar self-suggestion before asking for past-life interludes may be helpful in avoiding unpleasant reactions.

116

life impressions you have received, then you may begin to entertain the possibility that you are obtaining valid past-life information.

Most gratifying of all, of course, is the rare occasion when someone's past-life research can be verified by historical records confirming names, dates, places, etc. This degree of confirmation, though uncommon, occurs frequently enough among students of metaphysics to establish a reasonable validity to the existence of reincarnation. Despite the debunkers' assertions that an individual providing verifiable details must have subconsciously absorbed historic information—or, displaying the ability to speak another language, having become conversant in it—at some subconcious level during childhood, reasonable investigators have concluded otherwise. This has even gone beyond the esoteric realm of metaphysics; there now are practicing psychiatrists who are finding it beneficial to some patients to induce past-life recall and search it for incidents that may be crucial to certain psychological problems in this lifetime. To this extent, at least, there is a practical reality to the concept of reincarnation.

If a belief in reincarnation can be confirmed by relating past-life information to known historical data, another belief is confirmed in the process: anything tending to prove that an individual possesses memories of previous lives also tends to prove that something of man's personality—his memories, at least—do in fact survive physical death.

One other point: if it can be shown beyond reasonable doubt to exist, all the outraged denials of reincarnation by even the most established and respected religious doctrines can't change the fact. He who hath ears, let him hear.

Chapter 9

WHO'S KEEPING SCORE?

It is one thing for the human mind to extract from the phenomena of nature the laws which it has itself put into them; it may be a far harder thing to extract laws over which it has no control. It is even possible that laws which have not their origin in the mind may be irrational, and we can never succeed in formulating them.

—Sir Arthur Stanley Eddington
Space, Time, and Gravitation

The general consensus seems to be, "I'll be relieved when I get through *this* life; I certainly don't want to come back to another one like it." This still puzzles me. I simply can't identify with the gloomy attitudes toward this life experience. I've been knocking around this reality in the flesh for decades, now, and I just don't find it a tribulation. I'm not anxious to reach the end of my allotted sojourn here, and—if reincarnation is a fact, and I am to return—I presently feel no reluctance to do so.

My experiences include many of the trials and burdens that are commonplace in Western society. Family disruption during childhood, moving from pillar to post through adolescence, surviving depression and war, rearing children, suffering divorce, single-parenting, changing careers, being eluded by affluence, resisting governmental big-brotherism—the list of struggles can go on and on. On the other hand, I've always felt particularly fortunate in the blessings that *count*: foremost, good health; intelligence; education; healthy and intelligent children; consistent income for essentials, even if luxuries often must wait; one beneficial marriage and one great one; the ability to find challenge and satisfaction in many endeavors; and at least six decades without a crushing tragedy among those near and dear. In my estimation, these far outweigh the routine burdens and frustrations of getting from here to there.

I suppose my secret it that I've found life to be *interesting*. Uneventful and sedentary though it is in the eyes of others, my life experience has kept me entertained and challenged, and has never burdened me beyond my ability to cope. It has allowed time and space to let curiosity explore, speculations germinate, and concepts grow, as this book evidences. Perhaps happiness can be only a sometime thing, but enduring satisfaction and contentment can come from endless fascination, interest, and anticipation in one's life. I think I'd enjoy another time around.

If I have a choice. But it may be that many of us *must* come around again, even if we'd prefer not to. That, at least, is a tenet of the concept of *Karma*, a corollary to the concept of reincarnation and the subject of this chapter. It's difficult, controversial, and challenging, but the subject can't be omitted from any discourse that includes reincarnation.

Borrowed from Hindu mysticism, the original Sanskrit meaning of Karma is *literature*, or *work*. To the extent that one's lifetime of deeds and misdeeds leaves its mark on the fabric of the universe, one indeed authors a "work." This and the seeds one sows comprise one's Karma, as the word is defined in metaphysics. When used in this sense, the word usually is capitalized.

But Karma is more than a file in the Akashic Records (see footnote, p. 259); it's said to be a balance sheet of debits and credits that dogs an individual from one lifetime to the next—an extension of "as ye sow, so shall ye reap" to a cosmic time frame. It's the universal law of cause and effect. If this is accurate, it means you can't escape the consequences of your mistakes by dying.[1] According to the precepts of reincarnation, a major reason that most of us return repeatedly to mortality is to face again those kinds of situations wherein our past performance was found wanting. It seems that a lesson unlearned will be encountered again; if not in this life, then in another. Hard-line Karma proponents also insist that we return to suffer at the hands of others exactly those injustices and injuries

[1] However, an untimely or excruciating death may of itself discharge some karmic debt, unless it is by your own hand or of your own volition.

121

that we inflicted on them previously. Sometimes the exact others, reincarnated, whom we offended before.

Those who find this concept of Karma unpalatable point to the ostensible injustice it imposes. It hardly seems fair that I must pay in this lifetime for errors of a past one when I have no conscious knowledge of having committed them. How can I—the mortal I—learn from mistakes I don't even remember? Or why should I suffer for the past misdeeds of "some-one else," which I was, on the mortal level, in any previous life. If there is a just God, how can I believe in the concept of Karma as it's customarily taught? How can I reconcile the apparent contradiction of a just God imposing an unjust punishment? It is this that prompts many to disbelieve in Karma and its concomitant reincarnation.

These are valid, rational questions, and I have yet to find fully satisfactory answers. Still, we are told by practically all higher sources that Karma of some sort is indeed a law of the universe; whether we like it or not and whether we accept it into our belief systems or not, it exists and every mortal is subject to it. Obscure though they may be, there must be good—and just—reasons for the imposition of the law of Karma, and we certainly are free to speculate on them and on the way Karma works.

Apparently the whole thing started when a considerable number of Spirits followed the whims of their rather undisciplined free wills down paths leading away from perfection in which they were created. If we view God for the moment in the traditional religious concept as a singular, omnipotent entity, it follows that He is perfect. This follows logically because, being all-powerful, it is *His* concept of perfection, not yours or mine, that is imposed on us as a universal definition. It also follows that He hardly would define perfection in a way to make Himself imperfect. Thus, when He dissociated elements of Himself to become discrete Spirits, they also were perfect by His cosmic standards. Just as a small section cut from a holographic negative is said to contain all the elements of the image recorded in the whole film, each Spirit was identical in knowledge and values to God Himself.

Now, Cayce tells us God created the Spirits for His companionship. But identical clones of one's self certainly would not be stimulating companions, so God elected to give the Spirits free will and send them forth to experience individually the universe, materiality, and each other. Then, in due time, they would return to Him with their diversely developed personalities to merge into a Godhead community of stimulating companionship for the rest of eternity. Or at least until They (It?) elected to undertake new forms of creation.

Thus the initial intent of the Spirits was ultimate return to the Godhead, but unfortunately, the very free will necessary for the development of uniqueness led to some attitudes and activities that are unacceptable to the God-community. Just as in our mortal society there is an allowance of—and a need for—a variety of personalities, viewpoints, and talents, but a rejection of those with socially unacceptable characteristics, so it is above. The ''Ruling

Body'' of the universe cannot embrace Spirits whose motivations and endeavors are inimical to the plan of God.

We may know little about socially unacceptable actions on the higher levels, but it appears that the physical realm became a major stumbling block. Intended to be an enriching but transitory experience, mortal life proved so enticing to many Spirits that they procrastinated, lingering on to revel in the fleshly delights of the physical. Entering life forms already extant and savoring the experience, some indulged their whimsy by creating new or hybrid creatures that were ill-suited to independent physical existence upon withdrawal by the inhabiting Spirits. This of itself was imperfection, a perversion of the creative powers inherited by the Spirits from God; more onerous, perhaps, was their digression from their circular path back to God.

So it was decreed by the Heavenly Hierarchy of the time that the physical experience henceforth would occur only within narrow constraints. No longer would Spirits be allowed to create experimental living creatures, although they would retain the ability (in their mortal form) to create nonliving artifacts. Neither would a Spirit any more slip into and out of physical creatures like donning and then discarding a suit of clothes; once electing to enter, there would be one part of a Spirit that would—as a rule—''wear'' that physical raiment for the duration of that mortal experience. And gone was the freedom to enter just any fauna or flora striking a Spirit's fancy; an apelike animal then in existence was quickly refined to serve as the sole physical vessel for the Spirit's mortal experiences.[2] Thus, we are told, did early physical man emerge transcendent to the teeming life on earth, sanctified as the chosen mortal temple of the Spirit and its corpuscle of God. It is this sanctification, not some accident of blind evolution, that distinguishes man from the rest of the animals.

With these new conditions came another that was vastly more restrictive: that aspect or corpuscle of the Spirit designated to "wear" the physical body would be a separate consciousness—a separate aspect of mind—estranged from, and generally unaware of, the parent Spirit's higher consciousness. Heretofore the Spirits had occupied mortal creatures with full superconscious awareness, but this was changed with the advent of physical man; fledgling man was to perceive himself as a singular, temporal being, given one finite interval in which to perfect his experience. With awareness limited to the physical senses and with the apparent finality of death, mortals who were disposed to define and seek perfection on this level dared not waste time on self-indulgent digressions.

But why should a being of such limited awareness seek—or even conceive of—self-improvement? To our knowledge, no other creatures consciously strive to surpass the status quo or work toward conceptual ideals; only man seeks to mold his physical and social environment to conform to some abstract ideal. This single distinction, this

---

[2] We have been told of one exception: the dolphin has been selected (or designed) as a perfect vehicle for the Spirits to experience the unique physical world beneath the seas.

quantum leap in self-awareness beyond that of other creatures cannot be rationally accounted for by conventional theories of evolution. Then what explains it?

We understand it to be the Spirit within man that creates this distinction, for the mortal intellect is an aspect of Spirit mind. While conscious awareness normally is blocked from explicit memories and intellectual processes residing in the Superconscious, the conscious mind of the mortal nevertheless is susceptible to subtle influence by the higher self. Nuances of feeling, reaction, desire, drive, intuition, conscience—all of these can be "planted" by the Superconscious into the conscious mind upon occasion. Since the conscious mind has its own free will, the mortal individual is free to deny, ignore, consider, or act upon these higher influences at will but, being usually so subtle that we take them for products of conscious thought processes, these Spirit-directed innuendoes often are incorporated into our conscious rationales. Thus man is motivated to conceive of and seek out something beyond the status quo. The obvious fact that man has not progressed as a unanimous whole toward an exalted society is a result of several factors: subtle nudges form higher sources are filtered through the conscious mind and colored by conscious-mind prejudices and proclivities; the Spirits in their free wills perceive differing routes to their goal; not all Spirits are motivated toward noble ends; and many humans idolize rationality to the point of total rejection of intuitive perceptions.

So mankind blunders haltingly along the road of progress, marching to a multitude of drummers. And perhaps suffering along the way for errors of past lives of which we are unaware.

Would it make more sense if everyone were born with total conscious recall of previous lives? Would we not make greater progress by building on remembered experiences and past lessons instead of starting each lifetime from ground zero? Would it not be easier to accept the burdens of karmic obligations if we knew their causes? While the answers may be yes from our mortal viewpoint, it obviously is seen differently at the spiritual levels. As Eddington said in this chapter's opening quotation, we may never succeed in formulating rational laws for some phenomena, so the rationale behind Karma and reincarnation may be forever obscure. However, I believe the Creator and His universe are supremely logical, and that what may appear irrational is only a perception flawed by incomplete knowledge or information. There must be sound reasons for our birth in ignorance.

Perhaps it is because the principal objective of the mortal experience is to learn constructive use of that which is both our great attribute and great weakness: free will. To discipline our mortal free wills away from directions inimical to humankind. To align our wills with that of the Godhead—not in fear of retribution, but through each mortal's innate desire to live up to lofty ideals. For when you are *inwardly* motivated to find personal satisfaction in attitudes and activities beneficial to humanity, you will direct your free will in concert with God's.[3]

When you allow unbridled free will to impel you toward socially negative values and actions, defined as those directly or indirectly detrimental to other individuals or society in general, you are using your free will negatively. *It is this destructive use of free will that we are to outgrow,* even if it takes several lives filled with karmic lessons, if we are to eventually regain the original goal of mutual companionship within the Godhead.

There is a crucial factor in this: true growth involves *inner* values and attitudes; the development of personal ideals through which you voluntarily reject socially detrimental thoughts and actions that you otherwise might embrace in the exercise of undisciplined, ego-centered free will. Adherence to a code only from fear of external punishment or expectation of external reward, even though it may benefit society, does not uplift your character.

Developing innate discipline of will is a growth process. During the years of immaturity, a child must be constrained by externally imposed codes of conduct, but the parents, if they perceive their true role in rearing, will endeavor through example and reason to guide the child to positive inner values of his own. One who has reached chronological adulthood without a firm structure of inner values—whose outward demeanor is governed only by

---

[3]The practical purpose of all major religions is to inspire the individual to *feel*—and therefore to practice—love, respect, and justice for all humankind sharing this mortality. I think we can safely conclude that this reflects God's will.

the strictures of formal law and social convention—is nevertheless immature. He also is frustrated by the perception that his free will is thwarted by external restrictions, and it is characteristic of the human animal to chafe under restriction of free will. From this comes either unhealthy repression of personality or eruptions of socially destructive actions.

Psychologists long ago recognized the detrimental effect on mental and emotional balance of the subversion of free will to external expectations, and they responded with "do your own thing." While this may be emotionally cathartic for the individual, it is not so for society if "your own thing" is based on inappropriate or undefined and unrefined inner values. From society's viewpoint, after all, conformance to a consistent external structure of acceptable behavior is preferable to the chaos resulting from multitudes of individuals indiscriminantly exercising their unbridled free wills and doing an infinitude of their "own things."

Recognizing the need for social structure, the early churches imposed external rules through promised reward or punishment—Heaven or Hell—and most of them haven't refined their psychology since. Yet nearly two thousand years ago, Christ recognized the need to "do your own thing" and the psychological unsuitability of externally imposed "Thou shalt not" rules, and He sought to inspire, rather than command. When He said, "You have heard it said, 'Thou shalt not commit adultery,' but I say that he who looketh upon a woman with lust hath already committed adultery in his heart," He was urging us to embrace inner values that discourage even the thoughts of socially negative actions. To intentionally elevate our very thoughts, in fact, for "As ye think, so shall ye become." I believe this exhortation to develop socially positive structures of innate thought is the singular most important tenet of Christ's ministry. This is why He preached universal love, for love of fellow man automatically leads one to exalted inner values.

Given constructive inner values, free will becomes both disciplined and unfettered. Now if that seems contradictory, consider that free will is simply your freedom to make decisions and take actions consonant with your own desires—and when your *desires* are disciplined, your free will follows suit.

Now, what has all this to do with knowledge or ignorance or karmic obligations? Simply this: a knowledge of past karmic involvements inevitably would be perceived as "external" pressures that would prove inimical to development of disciplined free will in this lifetime; therefore that knowledge is denied to most of us at the conscious level.

There are several ways in which knowledge of one's Karma could influence present actions and value formations; perhaps even as many ways as there are people:

1. In the matter of karmic debt, perceived as having been incurred by a past-life offense against one whose Spirit may now be incarnate in someone of your present ac-

quaintance, you may consciously strive to make restitution out of fear of his reprisal. Conversely, if the past-life offense was against "you," you may be motivated by resentment to seek retaliation against the perpetrator's present-life counterpart. Neither fear of reprisal nor desire to retaliate is conducive to raising your consciousness in this life.

2. Another individual may be obligated to you for a past-life favor. Given knowledge of this, you might be tempted to consciously seek return of that favor, the expectation of reward influencing your attitudes and actions—and distorting your values and decisions.

3. Some persons misperceive the fruits of Karma as the fabric of predestination and simply resign themselves to "fate." This attitude is fatal to the very concept of free will.

4. Foreknowledge of the identities of those you are to meet again, and of your past-life relationships to them, can lead to inappropriate overtures. For example, knowledge that one newly encountered in this life was your lover in another incarnation certainly will color your interaction with that person today. We are charged with responding to others as they *are*, not as they were as some other mortal.

5. Awareness of Karma and reincarnation can cause some persons to procrastinate in

131

their development, much as was once the case with the Spirits before physical man. Why, one may reason, should I strive in this lifetime for edification when there appears to be an eternity of lifetimes? This may contribute to a philosophy of "enjoy now, pay later," extended over a cosmic time frame. This is not the way to enlightenment.

6. The concept of Karma is used by some as a cop-out. Every minor reversal of fortune, every slight affliction, every error of judgment is attributed to karmic harassment—perceived as a form of karmic punishment for past misdeeds. These individuals seem to believe that they would never make a mistake—make a wrong decision, trip over a rug, or catch a cold, if it weren't for their respective Spirit's continual imposition of petty karmic punishments. This attitude does little to encourage such persons to sharpen their judgment, develop agility, or mind their physical resistance to disease—but then why should it, when in their eyes they already would be perfect but for Karma?

All of these possible reactions to the conscious awareness of Karma can intrude on the process of developing one's inner value system and disciplining free will and, to the extent that they do, negate our purpose in this life. Ergo, it is decreed that most of us will enter physical life without conscious knowledge of previous lifetimes and the karmic imbalances we may bring with us. While it seems unjust by our limited logic to "owe" debts we don't know we incurred, it would be even less fair to bring with us a conscious burden that could delay—or even reverse—our intended progress toward that discipline of inner value and free will that ultimately will qualify us for return to residence within the Godhead.

What, then, of those of us who do entertain the concept of Karma? Does our awareness impede us on our path to enlightened discipline of will?

There is no singular answer. As with so many metaphysical matters, the impact of the knowledge of personal Karma varies with the individual. Many who are exposed simply reject it out of hand. This doesn't negate the influence of Karma on their lives, but their conscious decisions take no account of it. For these, awareness of the concept doesn't alter the paths they follow. This probably applies to a great majority of those in Western society, where belief in Karma isn't popular.

Some view Karma as a possible reality that is too abstract for them to discern its personal relevance, and they make no effort to incorporate the concept into their day-to-day decisions. These, too, are relatively unaffected by their knowledge. Others accept it as inscrutable fact, about which they can do little more than live "safely," incurring as little further karmic debt as possible, an attitude that can lead to inhibiton of free will by fear of retribution, which we have seen to be growth limiting.

Given acceptance of the concept of Karma, is there a "best" way to accommodate it? Again, that must be up to the individual. It's probably best if we can strike a balance—to understand the ways in which it may play a role in present-life activities, without becoming obsessed with countless past-life incidents that may have no real bearing on current problems and responsibilities. To this end, some progressive psychologists have found it beneficial to regress patients back to former lives in an effort to understand any incidents from those lives that may be contributing to their present psychological profiles. One of these is licensed clinical psychologist Allen Cohen, Ph.D., who told a seminar audience, " . . . sometimes, relationships are colored by past lives. And many of you have read . . . where other dynamics were going on that just can't be [explained] psychologically."[4] Dr. Cohen sometimes hypnotically regresses his patients to apparent past-life experiences, but prefers to work with a clairvoyant who has the ability to perceive others' past lives in considerable detail.

It would be helpful for putting it into perspective if we knew a little more about Karma. How rigidly is it imposed as the law of cause and effect? Are there alternative ways to "work off" karmic debts? Are there positive karmic benefits—good Karma, as some would have it? How does divine Grace enter in, if at all? These are questions on which there is no agreement among various proponents,

---

[4] At Northern Virginia Community College, Sterling, VA; March 27, 1982, at which time Dr. Cohen was Professor of Consciousness Studies at California's John F. Kennedy University.

so it's up to you once again to evaluate for yourself and accept only that which you find comfortable.

It is your own Superconscious that, in concert and mutual agreement with the SCs of other mortals with whom you interact, determines what your karmic burdens and rewards will be in this lifetime. You—the total, Spirit you—will have to face God's judgment years, centuries, or millennia from now, but it is the Superconscious aspect of you that is measuring the mortal, conscious part of you today, with the objective of having the total you in perfect karmic balance by the time of God's judgment.

Whatever your karmic legacy may be, and whatever your SC's rules of reward and punishment, you have the power to avoid adding any negative debt simply by living circumspectly from this moment on. But it's not enough to merely avoid wrongdoing out of fear of punishment (with its inhibition of free will); it takes positive and courageous effort to progress, and that's what it's all about. Good comes from a higher motivation than just abiding by the rules; it comes from inner values that make external rules unnecessary. Striving for it leads to inner growth, and also can offset some existing negative Karma if your Superconscious concurs. So my admonition is, don't withdraw and live in fear, but work aggressively toward inner growth for good, and let the Karma fall where it may. Leave it to your Superconscious to keep the score—and maybe you won't have to come back unless you want to. As for me, I believe I'd like to.

135

Chapter 10

TRANSITIONS

The heavens themselves, the planets, and the centre
Observe degree, priority, and place. . . .

—Shakespeare
Troilus and Cressida

Is there really an immortal aspect of man? What happens at physical death? Does one's consciousness go somewhere? If so, where? What's it like?

It was my childhood concept that upon death, one's soul or Spirit ascended immediately to the portals of Heaven, where it reported for one's personal Judgment Day. Then, provided one had lived an upstanding life, direct entry into Heaven was pretty much assured.

But Heaven, according to Sunday School, is some idyllic realm of existence where everyone has nothing to do all day but sit around and play harps. The prospect of this seemed utterly boring to me then, as it does now. Especially when you were going to be there for all eternity. Coupled with this view was the supposition that when a Spirit is liberated by death and enters the exalted realm of Heaven, it immediately becomes as omniscient as God, so there would be nothing left to learn, no mysteries to puzzle over, no achievements to strive for. In short, no objectives to occupy one's interest. Early on I concluded that either Heaven is no great reward, or death would have to effect a drastic change in my concept of what makes existence interesting.

Not that I considered Hell a preferable alternative. I didn't suppose a Spirit could feel ordinary fire and brimstone, so I assumed Hell must be a condition of intense emotional or psychological "heat" of some sort, imposed somehow by those entities in charge of eternal torment. This probably would be worse, though perhaps not much, than the endless boredom of Heaven.

However nobody seemed able to prove that there is a Heaven at all. But if so, is there anything to do there besides praise God and play a harp?

As I grew older, conventional Protestant churches did little to satisfy my inquiring mind in this matter, but other religious and metaphysical teachings offered concepts that were more tantalizing. The fact that most of these center on reincarnation—which I found difficult to accept—made them suspect in my eyes, but the glimpses they professed to give of purposeful activities occurring on nonmortal planes after death(s) certainly seemed more interesting than my conventional Heaven,

137

more comforting than utter finality, and more believable than resurrection of a past personality from nothing. It seemed inescapable, upon sufficient research into the literature, that disembodied consciousnesses of some sort do indeed manifest in various ways through some individuals. The question was, were these consciousnesses in fact the once-mortal personalities they claimed to be?

I find the concept of suspended existence pending Judgment Day to disagree with the apparent facts. As does instant transition to Heaven, Hell, or Purgatory[1] according to one's just reward. Our present understanding is that, although one who has worked through all his karmic lessons in his succession of mortal lives may go directly to Heaven (meaning to merge with the Godhead), most of us must anticipate and plan for further reincarnations. Since both Heaven and Hell (if it exists) are popularly understood to be final destinations, they are not likely habitats for Spirits preparing to reincarnate. It seems virtually certain, then, that there is a vast realm of nonmaterial reality apart from the "closed communities" of Heaven, Hell, Purgatory, Limbo, or whatever. Perhaps this realm is subdivided into several "astral planes," as some psychics describe, and is inhabited by beings of various stages of spiritual

---

[1]Certain of our Spirit sources proclaim that a level of existence called Purgatory does exist, although its function has never been articulated to my satisfaction. Others say there is no Purgatory; that the concept has been promulgated for the benefit of those whose belief structure is strengthened by it. This seems to lie behind many cases of conflicting concepts; there are various acceptable paths to the same goals, and their individual realities may be purely subjective.

development. According to Cayce, each Spirit must attain and master each of several "levels" or "dimensions of consciousness" in our solar system, and the planets represent those dimensions. Of the eight dimensions he defined, earthly physical experience represents the third one.[2] Whatever the astral structure, it seems evident that surviving personalities of mortals usually merge with their respective Spirits upon death and "go" to this realm, where they are active and from which they sometimes are accessible to those of us on this physical plane.

It's probably more accurate to say that the astral realm permeates the material realm and that surviving personalities don't "go" anywhere in the usual sense, but simply withdraw from physical manifestation into what may be but one of several dimensions of nonphysical reality. Mortals who are able to "project" their conscious awareness outside of their body seem to operate in an astral realm coinciding with physical reality but not constrained by natural physical barriers; presumably discarnate entities can operate there (here) as well.

There are conflicting clues regarding the "movements" of soul/Spirit aspects upon death. There are several well-documented books detailing anecdotal research into the perceptions of persons who have survived near-death experiences, a large proportion of whom had a sensation of traveling at

---

[2]According to Thomas Sugrue in *There Is a River* (Dell Publishing Co., 1945). The chapter titled "Philosophy" provides an excellent summary of the creation and evolution of the Spirits and of mortal mankind as portrayed by the Cayce readings.

high speeds through a dark tunnel or black nothingness toward an illuminated scene. At the far end, they variously encountered Christ, other religious figures either recognized or unidentifiable, deceased loved ones, or just an indescribable light with an overwhelmingly loving personality. In most cases, it seems, the entities they encounter are those by whom the particular individual may be best comforted during a traumatic incident, suggesting that the appropriate perceptions are arranged in one manner or another by the individual's own higher self.

The point of interest here, though, is the common sensation of motion—of traveling to some undefinable elsewhere. However, this seems to conflict with my wife, Marianne's, perceptions of soul/Spirit auras lingering in the physical plane following death: at funerals, she has perceived two distinct discarnate aspects of the deceased. These take the form of vaguely human-shaped luminosities, usually of the same hue but of different brightnesses. The one of lesser intensity is understood to be the "soul body" of the mortal—the nonphysical vehicle for the conscious memories and unique personality of the individual; the brighter is the "Spirit body." The auras are separate but remain close to one another as they appear in the sanctuary; then at some point during the sermon, the lesser aura simply merges with the greater one, which then manifests their combined luminosity and floats through the congregation to take up a position adjacent to the most bereaved (often the surviving spouse). It may appear near the bereaved for days or even weeks following its mortal's death.

This perception seems to confirm our concept of distinct conscious, mortal-level and superconscious, spiritual-level facets of the total human, and of the absorption by the Spirit of all mortal-level memories and personality patterns shortly after physical death. It doesn't confirm the sensation of traveling rapidly to elsewhere that is reported by many of those who have had near-death experiences; perhaps this is only the difference between subjective and objective views (if aura perception can be considered objective!) of the transition experience.

Thus far, then, we have deduced that at physical death, your consciousness does not become nonexistent.[3] Neither does it go into some state of suspended existence; yet it also does not—in most cases—go to "places" like Heaven, Hell, etc. Then do you simply float about on some barren astral plane, or even the physical plane, for years until time to reincarnate? Without even a harp to play? That would be even more boring than the stereotypical Heaven; there must be *something* to do!

If this seems simplistic, what it overlooks is the *rest* of you: your Spirit. Even during life, while

---

[3] As noted here, we have come to understand that the consciousness—the package of mortal memories and personality patterns that we have come to think of as the "soul"—merges at some time after death with the Superconscious, losing its uniqueness as an isolated identity. In this sense, it can be said to die, as the Bible insists the "soul" does at death. Yet all the memories and personality traits are preserved amongst the voluminous other data already resident in the Superconscious—the Spirit's mind—and are recallable at any time.

the conscious aspect of you is occupied with the activities of physical existence, your Spirit—the vehicle of your Superconscious—is functional at some astral level and engages in many activities beyond your mortal awareness. At some time after your transition, your then-discarnate conscious self will merge with your Spirit, much as Marianne has percieved with others. At that moment, the conscious you ceases to exist as the singular, limited personality you perceived yourself to be as a mortal; in that sense, you die. In effect, though, you are reborn (nonphysically) as an infinitely more varied, multifaceted individual integrating the aggregated experiences of all your mortal lifetimes.

Surprise: having integrated after death into a singular Spirit entity, you have duties to attend to! Most sources agree that you undergo a review (either introspectively or in dialogue with a Spirit mentor) to evaluate the effect of your most recent mortal sojourn on your higher goals and your karmic balance. This evaluation takes place somewhere in the astral realms.[4] Coupled with this is counseling and assistance by wise Spirits in plan-

---

[4] The "layout" of the astral realms is a subject of much disagreement between metaphysicists. Some insist on the traditional seven levels, with access to progressively higher ones being permitted only to equally progressively enlightened entities. Others assign as astral locations the various planets of our solar system, designating them as focal points for the various degrees of astral exaltation. Apart from the observation that apparently at least one level of astral activity coincides with the physical earth plane, I concern myself very little with their explicit restrictions and "locations"; I don't believe we can determine—or need—on this level more than a generalized idea of the *activities* to be encountered in the astral realm. The specifics will become evident when they are needed; that is, upon arrival "there."

ning your next undertaking, whatever it may be. Just to sample the general unanimity on this aspect of between-lives activity: Kaleb, an entity who manifests through automatic writing by Darlene Hopper, reports: "While resting between lifetimes, the soul [Spirit] assimilates the lessons of its previous life. . . . Here, one attends spiritual classes presided over by masters.[5] Seth[6] explains that, in this time of rest and choosing, all counsel is given. And Michael[7] says, " . . . There is much time for reflection and much guidance."

In view of my early supposition that, upon having crossed over into the celestial realms, one instantly became omniscient, able to perceive all truths and penetrate all mysteries, it's not surprising that I was shocked to learn that Spirits need to learn and grow, too. But that's what we're told by a large number of sources, including Cayce. For most of us, the physical experience is a necessary part of that learning and few master it all in one mortal lifetime.

It's long been commonplace for one who has stared imminent death in the face to report: "My whole life passed before my eyes." Some people say it was like a movie projecting that lifetime's

[5]*Direct from Spirit*, by Darlene Hopper. Valley of the Sun Publishing; 1983.
[6]Seth is the entity who spoke through the late Jane Roberts in trance. The Seth material is perhaps the most widely known among numerous published works purporting to originate with discarnate "higher" sources; not all of Seth—nor of most other such sources—is in accord with our understanding. *Seth Speaks*; Prentice-Hall; 1972.
[7]*Messages from Michael*, by Chelsea Quinn Yarboro, is a compilation of communications received via Ouija board by Jessica and Walter Lansing from an entity called Michael. Playboy Paperbacks; 1979.

events sequentially but in an inexplicably accelerated time frame—a fraction of a second; others claim they saw their whole life in one instantaneous flash. In some near-death experiences, this recalling of one's past occurs upon emergence from the far end of the "dark tunnel," often accompanied by awareness of a presiding entity there who invites review and the subject's *self*-evaluation of the lifetime without imposing any judgment of its own. This is in harmony with our understanding that whatever initial judgment there may be waiting at the end of a present lifetime is made by one's own higher self; that the ultimate judgment by God, Christ, or other exalted deity, if it occurs, will be of the total Spirit and the attributes of the composite character formed from *all* its mortal experiences, and lies somewhere beyond the end of one's final reincarnation.

Apparently there is more, though, than self-evaluation; for most of us there is school! Advisor Spirits are there to counsel you in refined techniques for nurturing of the "new leaf"—the blank area of sentience that will be your conscious mind in your next incarnation. And there are other details to attend regarding that incarnation: where, when, which sex, what parents, and what associated Spirits will most likely advance your own growth process in that physical experience? And are there demands for some of your attention remaining back on the physical plane you left? Perhaps you have a few decades of being some mortal's "guide," "guardian angel," or spiritual companion to discharge before you can even consider your own return.[8] Or it may even be that you have learned well from your succession of physical experiences and are yourself qualified to counsel other Spirits at some level, in which case you may be requested to serve in the guiding hierarchy for a few decades or centuries before moving on in your own development. And there is social inter-action and discourse among groups of Spirit friends, and perhaps some obligations that are be-yond our mortal comprehension. Whatever your lot in the astral interim, it has to be more interesting than playing a harp all day—or dodging fire and brimstone, if that should be the alternative.

As with any large group of individuals, there must be an effective organizational structure in the Spirit realms. We understand there to be a hier-archy of guiding entities and groups having various levels of responsibility in the usual pyramidal structure, with the Godhead as the capstone. I say *responsibility* in preference to *authority*, because authority implies the power to enforce conformity, which apparently is not currently wielded in the astral realm. Perhaps there is a practical reason for this: it's pretty difficult to imprison a nonmaterial entity, or to fine one, or to discontinue one's pay-check, so incentives for compliance that work on

---

[8] It is fairly commonplace for a sensitive to perceive an entity always present near an individual, apparently serving in some capacity as support (and perhaps companion) to the individual's own Spirit and sometimes even providing guidance in some form directly to the indi-vidual. Upon probing, it frequently is revealed that the entity is a deceased grandparent, although other former relatives, spouses, and sometimes just close friends also are found to serve as companion Spirits.

the mortal level may be totally ineffective in the astral realm.

More to the point, however, is the sacrosanct status of free will among Spirits. They were given free will at their creation and charged with learning to exercise it constructively. As we have seen earlier, any proscription of behavior by external constraints is deprivation of free will and interferes with a Spirit's potential growth, so forceful authoritarian coercion does not exist on these planes. If a Spirit fails to fulfill—or even recognize—an obligation to cooperate with the community, it is free to go its own errant way. It may receive censure or remonstrance from its more dedicated brethren, but it can always search out other irresponsible Spirits to associate with.

This, we understand, is not the way to Heaven, but some Spirits don't care. In fact, it's not surprising to learn that some Spirits go beyond indifference and irresponsibility so far as to rebel against the hierarchy, for ego and jealousy and desires for power and favor exist in Spirit minds, too. Individually, these Spirits are viewed by those who are in accord with God as being misguided; en masse, however, they can be a formidable force for evil.

Which involves us for a moment in the classical debate over good and evil. If in fact God exists and has a plan, good must be defined as any act or attitude in accord with His plan, and evil is any act or attitude inimical to that plan. To the extent that rebellious Spirits entice others to join them, they diminish the ranks and the unity of those endeavoring to further God's plan and therefore are evil.

146

More insidious, though, is the rebellious Spirits' influence in the physical world through their mortal incarnations, by which they disrupt the major objective of the physical experience: to learn to live in loving harmony with fellow humans. For it is on the earth plane that man is least aware of his spiritual heritage and most likely to err and stumble over roadblocks to spiritual progress; roadblocks which often are cleverly camouflaged in the guise of rationalism and "progress."

Among such roadblocks is the oft-quoted philosophy that "evil exists only in the minds of men." In essence, this philosophy denies any intellect greater than man's, leaving the definition of evil to some kind of mortal consensus that is subject to change as conditions, opinions and desire may dictate. This strips morality of its true significance, leaving its form to vacillate with the times and the undulating whims of society. It also puts man off his guard against subtle, directed evil, rendering him more vulnerable to the efforts of those whose very SCs are misguided.

Our spiritual sources reject this philosophy of evil being only a matter of mortal viewpoint. They paint instead a picture of highly organized and polarized factions on the astral plane that are vying for the uncommitted Spirits of mortal mankind. The rebellious faction is organized and dedicated to ultimately wresting the universe from God Himself, whereupon they expect to indulge in the spoils of the victor. The other faction, fiercely loyal to what they understand to be God's plan, are no less committed to victory.

147

If there is a unified group of rebellious Spirits, it follows that they, too, must have some organization. There must be levels of authority and a governing body to coordinate the whole. And most governing bodies have a singular individual at their apex, be he president, chairman of the board, premier, or king. In the case of celestial rebellion, a ringleader would have to possess supreme audacity to challenge the very throne of God, and there is only one Spirit in the universe who ever developed the monstrous ego to do so. He is known in the Bible by many names, but our spiritual sources most often refer to him as Lucifer, the fallen Angel of Light, who removed himself from God's favor eons ago. Notwithstanding the position of many philosophies denying the personification of evil and rejecting the idea of a spiritual entity with an organized following that is consciously seeking victims, it is our understanding that Lucifer and his Spirit minions are united in rebellion against those loyal to God; that indeed personified evil exists both within and beyond the minds of mortal man, and that final resolution of the conflict lies in the indefinite future. (It doesn't necessarily follow from this that there is a Hell.)

If our understanding is correct, then a picture of life in the astral realms emerges: they are peopled by at least two distinct factions, each with its own organization and allegiances. Apparently each can perceive the other, but communication between opposing group members is virtually nonexistent. At least it is our experience that a Spirit may freely exchange information with another of the ''good guys," but usually is unable to glean information from those of opposing allegiance; apparently they just aren't on "speaking" terms. (Which, if nothing else, seems to indicate that mental privacy exists even in realms where communication by telepathy—"mind reading"—is the norm. Yet we know from experience that entities from the negative side *can* communicate with us if they so elect and we permit.) There seems to be no overt warfare at this time on the other levels. Certainly no physical engagement, since noncorporeal beings are immune to injury; and apparently no mind warfare, as though the enlightened Spirits consider it too demeaning to even address themselves to any of the enemy.

This really isn't an "ignore them and they'll go away" attitude; it's simply deemed more effective for the long run to concentrate on supporting and guiding members of the loyal faction as they progress toward their ultimate goal. So the negative faction is effectively ignored while effort is devoted to the activities mentioned earlier: counseling and education of Spirits between incarnations, providing higher-source guidance to worthy mortals, interacting with the Superconsciouses of those Spirits currently incarnate, and serving as needed in appropriate capacities within the celestial hierarchy.

There must be some interesting differences from physical existence during life in the astral realm. For instance, there's the matter of time, which usually is said to be meaningless there. Meaningless it may be—or perhaps more accurately, simply indefinable—but certainly not nonexistent. We are

149

told there is a sequence of events; that one happening is observed to occur before the next one; that past, present, and future may be perceived by the Spirit, but never confused as would be the case if they were truly simultaneous. I suspect that time there is totally subjective, being dynamic or static as befits the activities of the entity involved. This would mean that two hundred years, say, between the end of one incarnation and a subsequent reincarnation may seem short, long, or moderate, depending on the characteristics and interim activities of the entity.

On the physical level, one way to eliminate the subjective flow of time is to sleep. This is one reason the animals were given sleep: to alleviate the sheer boredom that even animals can suffer during long periods of inactivity. Perhaps they suffer even more than we would, since we don't believe most of them do much thinking and daydreaming to pass away idle times. In any event, sleep shortens the long, dark night for the daytime feeder, and accelerates the unproductive daytime hours for the nocturnal beast. Secondarily, the lowered metabolism of sleep allows a degree of bodily rejuvenation among the animals, although it's long been known that sleep is not required for physical maintenance. Then along comes man, with a rational mind that is endlessly assaulted with sensory stimuli and busied with the myriad details of conscious activity, and the sleep function inherited from his animal ancestry comes to serve another purpose: as a temporary disengagement of his consciousness from sensory bombardment, necessary for reviewing and classifying the day's data as it relates to the historical data accrued from the mortal's birth, and then filing everything away in an associative matrix of memory. It also may, during the disengagement of sleep, interchange data and communication with other levels of mind, such as the Superconscious[9] and/or subconscious. While little is known of the actual mechanisms at work, science has determined that although sleep is not essential to survival of the body, it is necessary for maintenance of mental equilibrium.

But is this true of discarnate individuals? Do Spirits indulge in "sleep" either by necessity or choice? Can the passage of time in the astral realm be subjectively accelerated by curling up on some figment of the imagination and catching forty million winks? Or are they perpetually awake and mentally active? This is an area we've never specifically addressed, and it may not be important to us while we're here in physical reality, but we do understand that *in*carnate Spirits often engage in numerous far-flung activities while their respective mortals sleep, particularly during the years of physical childhood. These include some of our own formerly discarnate sources who manifest to us upon particular occasions while the mortal aspects of their new incarnations sleep, from which we

---

[9]Some metaphysicists contend that a person is undertaking astral travels, or traveling outside the body, during much of his sleep time, or at least during the dream intervals. This may be true of some individuals, but we believe it is not representative for most of us. Communication with the SC, evidenced by problem-solving or accurately prophetic dreams, occasionally takes place—again, the frequency is dependent on the particular individual.

might reasonably infer that sleep isn't necessary at the superconscious level.

But recreation is. "All work and no play" is as deadly at the superconscious as at the conscious level, so the counseling, planning, guiding, and other duties with which one is charged during discarnate interludes are interspersed with pleasure activities—whatever they may be at that level. Many Spirits must enjoy social discourse with their circle of friends, and the ability to create practically anything one might desire surely permits a variety of recreational experiences. Creation of subjective reality in the nonphysical realms is simply a matter of thought-forms. If it happened that one actually wanted a heavenly harp, he needs merely to visualize it—to "dream" it; he can create it and then play it with all the subjective reality of an earthly harp, but only he and those others who choose to do so will hear him play. Sort of the best of two worlds in a cosmic sense!

Having discoursed here at length about life in the astral realm, it must be apparent that we really don't know much about it. We can speculate; we can assert that there is noncorporeal existence there, and it seems fairly safe to accept that one's intervals of discarnate existence include a lot of learning and counseling and planning. Beyond this and our understanding that there are indeed factions of two opposed loyalties resident there, we really don't have much emphasis given by our sources to the details of life between lives. This, we may conclude, is because those details are not important to us during our physical experience; it is our mortal here-and-now existence and how we cope with this life on the conscious level that are of the most immediate importance.

Chapter 11

KALEIDOSCOPE OF THE PARANORMAL

This world, after all our science and sciences, is still a miracle; wonderful, inscrutable, magical and more, to whoever will think of it.

—Thomas Carlyle

A kaleidoscope uses colorful fragments of glass or stone having a variety of shapes and apparently unrelated origins, and illuminates them in fascinating, animated patterns that are mostly illusory reflections from internal mirrors. And so it is with things paranormal, occult, psychic, metaphysical, or whatever you wish to call them: colorful, fascinating, seemingly unrelated, and highly illusory. But among the multiple patterns of the kaleidoscope image there is one real one—one arrangement of actual fragments, the appearance of which is exaggerated by several mirror reflections. The same can be said, I believe, for the many facets and illusions of paranormal phenomena: there are underlying truths to be discerned among their evident patterns. In this chapter, we'll discuss several facets of the paranormal in the context of what we understand about the activities and powers of our higher selves.

This may strike you as a puzzling digression. After so many chapters ranging from "personal reality" to personal sanctity, leaping into the kaleidoscopic arena of "far-out" psychic/metaphysical phenomena may appear to be jumping the track. To the contrary, however; the hypothesis that ties all these outwardly different manifestations to the essential premise of this book is the existence of the superconscious mind. But the assertions made in this chapter are simply food for thought. As always, you must weigh the evidence and decide for yourself.

There is such a broad variety of phenomena ascribed to the psychic or paranormal that I can't address all of them here. Among those that I do elect to touch upon, perhaps the best one to start with is *intuition*.

Intuition is a process of reaching valid conclusions without linear, logical reasoning. It is stereotypically assumed to be more prevalent in women than in men; this may be true, but everyone has the potential to be intuitive if only they will "listen" to their inner selves.

I don't doubt that many intuitive perceptions and conclusions involve nothing more than the conscious and/or subconscious levels of mind. However, we understand that the "intuitive flash" of knowledge often is imparted by the *Super*conscious in what is probably the most common and subtle means of communication from the higher self. To this extent, then, intuition is a psychic manifestation; a communication from the nonphysical domain of the Superconscious. It's probably accurate to say that intuition is the mechanism by which psychic perceptions are planted in the conscious mind. Men are no less endowed with superconscious minds than are women and therefore are potentially as physically intuitive; yet it seems true that, among those who are "sensitive" to psychic input, women outnumber men by a substantial ratio. Probably we men have just habituated ourselves more to discounting and denying the nonrational.

By ascribing the source of some intuitive insights to the SC, and further declaring the mechanism of intuition to be the channel through which many psychic perceptions manifest, we imply that the SC is somehow involved in those events we consider psychic.

Mental telepathy—mind reading—is one psychic function that can be readily explained in terms of communication at the superconscious-mind level. Others construct elaborate theories involving transmission and reception of some radiolike energy to account for mind-to-mind communication, but the radio analogy fails to support the observed characteristics of telepathy. Unlike radio transmission, telepathy seems essentially unaffected by distance or any form of electrical interference, and enclosing a "sender" or "receiver" in a Faráday cage, which is an effective barrier to radio propagation, apparently doesn't diminish mental communication in the least. Further, there has yet been no discovery of scientifically verifiable psychic energies or "vibrations" generated by the "sender" having sufficient power to cover global distances, at least within our understanding of the natural laws of signal transmission.[1]

Another hypothesis supposes an all-pervasive medium, such as the "ether" of nineteenth-century science, in which a minute disturbance such as might be caused by the mind of a sender is propagated like ripples in a pond and is sensed by a receiver who is attuned to the particular vibrations of the sender. This seems to require that less power be generated by the sender than does the radiolike hypothesis, but it is equally unverified.

There is a much simpler explanation, if you accept that you have a higher consciousness that can communicate with other similar Superconsciouses independently of your conscious mind, and that it

---

[1]The Soviets, recognizing that telepathy is a fact, are seeking an understanding of it in materialistic terms. They postulate a "bio-energy" to be generated, modulated, and directed by life forms and in fact they seem to be measuring bio-energy emanations. However, the power levels they evidently are detecting are extremely small and surely can't propagate over great distances.

can do so in nonphysical realms unhampered by time and distance. It only takes willing contact between the SCs of the telepathic sender and receiver, and attunement of the receiver's conscious mind to his Superconscious, for the message to arrive. There is no problem here of energies, distances, or interference. Of course this replaces the question of how telepathy occurs in our physical world with the larger and perhaps more obscure question of how the Spirits communicate in the astral realms, but if one accepts as a working reality that they *do* communicate—perhaps as integral elements of an all-pervasive Universal Consciousness—then this concept of a mechanism for mental telepathy seems more straightforward than those more convoluted ones requiring creation and/or propagation of some mysterious and as-yet-undiscovered physical energies, vibrations, etc.

Another psychic activity said to involve the Superconsciouses of two individuals is *hypnosis*. This is a rather broad term used for exercising the power of suggestion at mind levels ranging from the fully conscious to deep, unconscious trance. While it is possible and can be beneficial to engage in self-hypnosis, we are concerned here with the more conventional concept of two participants: hypnotist and subject.

An elementary form of light hypnosis can be involved in something as commonplace and inescapable as advertising. To the extent that an advertiser can invoke the power of suggestion to influence your choice of products, however subtly, he is using hypnosis. Preachers and politicians use intonations and inflections that can have some hypnotic effect on their audiences. At a more sinister level, an analysis of Adolf Hitler's speaking mannerisms in public speeches has led some to believe that he may have exercised a remarkably hypnotic influence over his audiences.

Increasingly, hypnosis is being used by dentists to suggest away their patients' sensation of pain, and some psychologists use hypnosis in their quest to uncover the buried traumas contributing to their patients' problems, or to plant suggestions to break old habits. But of course the popular conception is of the stage hypnotist who, with a full complement of gesticulations and incantations, puts his willing subjects through hilarious antics that they fail to recall upon being ''brought out'' of trance. That one person could so completely control another who is unconscious seems almost like magic.

My first exposure to anything beyond self-hypnosis was a demonstration at a seminar. I watched and listened closely to the demonstrator, a practiced and professional hypnotist, as he put a volunteer into trance to regress her to certain childhood incidents. There was no mumbo-jumbo, no ''Look into my eyes. . . . you now are in my power,'' no mellifluous intonation of voice. He spoke simply, directly, conversationally, with a rustic accent, holding one of her hands and having her concentrate her gaze on an ordinary wooden pencil. While she did not go into a deep trance, she did deem the regression successful.

I pondered this with fascination. I was confident that I could have done exactly as the hypnotist outwardly did, without achieving the slightest success. I concluded from this that there had been some unperceived communication between hypnotist and subject; that something like mental telepathy had taken place. What, I wondered, did the hypnotist possess that made this happen?

According to one concept offered by the Jupiter Movement, the degree of "control" allowed the hypnotist is *always* determined by the subject's higher self; therefore, if we assume that an SC isn't susceptible to deception, there should be no real risk in undergoing hypnosis, since your own SC presumably is protecting your interests.

There are those who disagree; who perceive hypnosis as "opening" your mind to control by another who may not have your best interests at heart. Or, as a further theory goes, once you have allowed someone to "enter your mind" via hypnosis, you have opened a breach in your mental defenses that may subsequently allow entry by wrongly motivated entities.

This whole area of hypnosis remains unclear. There are so many levels of hypnotic "trance," and there are so many obscure corners of the subconscious, conscious, and superconscious minds which manifest in various ways under hypnosis, that I am not prepared at this time to propound a specific mechanism. Even professional hypnotists widely disagree in their concepts of the way it works. But my observation and experience lead me to believe that there *is* some kind of nonverbal and nonphysical coercion—however benevolent it may be—wielded by the hypnotist (or his SC), and I know that information given by a subject in hypnotic trance isn't always factual, even though it may seem so to the subject. Hypnosis is an area of metaphysics that you might like to approach with caution, but not with fear.

Another metaphysical manifestation that ordinarily involves two persons is *induced healing*. Whether you call it faith healing, psychic healing, miracle cure, or whatever, there are individuals who are able upon occasion to act as catalyst in the supernormal healing of another. In a field fraught with charlatans and sincere but deluded practitioners, there are some whose talents I deem to be genuine. One of the better known of the recent era was the late Olga Worrell, who spent a lifetime as an instrument of psychic healing. She, like most legitimate "healers," denied that she possessed any inherent powers; she said only God can heal. Somehow, she believed, she was able to guide or entice His healing power to enter an afflicted individual and effect a cure.

Or the late Reverend Kathryn Kuhlman, who in the late 1940s emerged from a small ministry in Franklin, Pennsylvania, to become a northside Pittsburgh institution of worldwide prominence. Literally thousands of crutches abandoned by attendees who experienced healings at her service adorned the walls of her meeting halls, attesting to her ability to invoke what she believed to be God's healing powers.

Some persons believe that there is a vast pool of psychic energy that is neutral; i.e., it's simply *there*. Having no more inherent affinity for good or evil than does gravity or sunlight, this energy can be manipulated by those who have the knack, for good *or* evil purposes as the manipulator may direct. In this view, psychic healers aren't catalysts for the healing power of God, but are utilizing unrecognized talents of their own in actually imparting curative properties to neutral psychic energy and directing it into the afflicted person's body.

The obverse of this healing concept is that the same neutral power can be used for negative purposes, such as invoking curses on individuals. There are today a number of books, programs, and courses purporting to teach you how to shield yourself from psychic attacks or curses, and of course folklore is rife with charms and rituals to ward off the "evil eye" and other outside psychic influences. However, even though the literature is full of curse legends, and serious research into the ability of one individual to psychically influence another is continuing, our experience to date suggests that supernormal healing—which does occur—and the devastation of a curse, if it truly is possible, are not opposite sides of the same mechanism.

Understanding the mechanism of supernormal healing is complicated by the fact that we really don't understand "normal" healing. What are the energies involved in, say, healing a cut finger? How are they directed? How do the cells involved "know" the forms and positions required to close the wound?

We're just beginning to learn at the crudest experimental level that externally applied electric and magnetic fields can influence tissue and bone regeneration. What natural healing "energies" are these fields supplementing or stimulating? Is it possible that a psychic healer can in fact manipulate healing energies? Or is it that the healer, like the hypnotist, has some influence with the SC of the subject to be healed and that it is the SC that actually directs the physical body's response?

What *is* behind paranormal healing? Is there some universal "psychic" energy that is wielded or manipulated by the gifted healer? Or is it the power of God, or of the healer?

Again, there are no clear-cut answers. There do seem to be energies of some kind involved. Kirlian photographs reveal marked differences in the energy distributions around psychic healers' finger tips when they are actively sending out healing "vibes" as compared to their ordinary states (see footnote, p. 173). Some sensitives can perceive (or are psychically shown) an intensified auralike emanation from the hands of a healer when he is active. And the recipients of such healing frequently describe sensations of "heat," or "vibrations," or some other energylike manifestation. Whether all these represent manipulation of some neutral, all-pervasive "astral" energy, or a focusing of energy inherent to the healer himself on either the superconscious or conscious level, or perhaps a directing of divine healing energy is open to conjecture. What does seem acceptable is that all healing, at whatever level, actually is performed by the recipient's physical body, possibly utilizing some form of energy or influence that we can't yet define. It may be that this healing energy does come directly from God, or other divine essence; but even if one's own SC—not to mention a healer's SC—is instrumental in influencing the state of the physical body, then by virtue of the SC's own "corpuscle of God," the healing comes ultimately from the Creator.

Supernatural healing doesn't always require two individuals—at least two mortal ones; some persons experience healing dreams or visions. M. E. Penny Baker in her book *Meditation: A Step Beyond with Edgar Cayce*[2] recounts her 1970 experience with a deep duodenal ulcer. Upon their examination of X-rays, two doctors concurred on her need for immediate medical treatment. She was prescribed the usual dietary prohibitions and alleviative medications, which she found intolerable and failed to follow. During this preoccupation with physical problems, Baker had neglected her customary daily meditation. About ten days later, she found herself in what she describes as the worst pain she has ever experienced, and she felt a mysteriously strong compulsion that night to go into deep meditation. She says, " . . . it was almost as if a power beyond my conscious control took over."

During the night, she became aware of the comforting presence of a dearly beloved friend who had

---

[2] In Chapter XII: "Healing." N.Y.: Pinnacle Books, 1975.

been dead for fifteen years. She received repeated assurances from him that all would be well, and she awoke in the morning "feeling marvelous." From that time forward, she had no further symptoms, even though she still ate, smoked, and imbibed as self-indulgently as ever. She did pray and meditate deeply every night. Three weeks after this episode, she returned for follow-up X-rays and, when the examining physician couldn't see her ulcer on the fluoroscope, he hastily retrieved the X-ray plates from her previous session for comparison. In the end, X-rays proved conclusively that the deep ulcers visible in the first session had completely disappeared by the second one, taken just thirty days later.

Penny Baker states that she does not think the deceased friend who appeared to her on that miraculous night was the healing agency, but was there as a trusted figure to reassure her so that her conscious mind could clear a channel to accept what was happening. She ascribes the actual healing to her concentrated meditation and whatever agencies and energies she may have influenced thereby. In other words, do-it-yourself healing. If in fact the SC is instrumental in healing its mortal, then do-it-yourself may be an appropriate label.

This is but one instance of many that seem to show that supernormal healing can be accomplished through effort by the subject himself. Self-hypnosis, visualization, prayer, repetitive affirmation—all of which may be nothing more than various names for the same underlying mechanism—have been used with varying degrees of success. Even formal medicine now is beginning to experiment with visualization, in which the patient is instructed how to picture his body tissues and defenses to be whole and invulnerable to invasion by the enemy pathogen or malignancy or whatever. Some participants seem to hasten a victory over disease, or to trigger a remission, or achieve some other benefit not normally accountable for in orthodox medical texts. Whether these solo methods encourage the patient's Superconscious to expedite healing, or "program" the subconscious, or open channels to outside healing influences on the astral level is a matter of conjecture, but they demonstrate at some level the power of mind over body. Since we accept the SC as the highest level of man's mind, it seems reasonable to credit it with the power either to perform or to initiate and oversee the healing process.

This is not a put-down of conventional medicine. While the medical fraternity, like other sciences, is steeped in custom and is suspicious of the unorthodox, in balance medicine is a great benefactor to mankind. Enlightened doctors recognize that their drugs and remedies don't really heal; they assist the body to heal itself. But what few realize is that the best among them have within themselves some talent for psychic or supernormal healing. The puzzling difference in success rates sometimes noted between two doctors of comparable knowledge, skill, and technique lies in the fact that one inherently has an astral "license" to encourage healing at the superconscious level, while the other—however nobly intentioned at the conscious-mind level—is limited to the accomplishments of a skilled technician.

We need doctors. Those who expect God to meet all their healing needs tend to overlook the fact that His ways are many and mysterious, and that the ministrations of the medical community are one of the tools at His disposal. To spurn professional medical attention to serious health problems is to close one avenue through which He may manifest. On the other hand, "The Lord helps those who help themselves"; perhaps if we were to better understand the real prime mover of all physical healing, the Superconscious (with its corpuscle of God, remember), we could usually "heal" ourselves unaided in all but the most dire afflictions.

Turning now to psychic abilities usually experienced in an individual context, *clairvoyance* is a technique of perceiving objects, people, or scenes at a distance beyond the perceiver's normal visual reach. A variation is *clairaudience*, the perceiving of sounds (usually human speech) beyond reach of the perceiver's physical auditory sense. These terms usually apply to abilities that don't require a "sender." In this sense, they do not include the "remote viewing" abilities explored by Targ, Puthoff, Harary, and others at SRI International, in which "senders" proceeded to selected geographical sites and attempted to send images to "receivers" who then drew sketches of images that came into their minds. This is an aspect of telepathy; the practice of clairvoyance is understood to involve only the clairvoyant.

Again, the capabilities of the Superconscious can easily account for this talent, if in fact the SC can instantaneously "visit" or focus on any physical location and can employ its own independent faculties of perception, which it seems to do. All that's required is a cooperative SC and attunement to its input by the seeker's conscious mind, and you potentially have a clairvoyant. As with most psychic endeavors, the better the "channel" of communication from SC to conscious mind, the more accurate and detailed are the perceptions.

There is confusion in some metaphysical doctrines between clairvoyance and out-of-body, or astral, travel. By our understanding, some aspect of the SC functions within astral realms at all times and, instead of traveling, it merely focuses attention wherever it pleases in what we perceive on the conscious level to be a physical locale. In this framework, it is erroneous to look upon "astral travel" as exceptional, and to mistake the often-symbolic clairvoyant input from the SC as literal, conscious-mind perception. Based on my wife, Marianne's experiences, genuine out-of-body astral travel involves a separation from the physical body of the *mortal-level*, everyday consciousness, not the free-roaming SC. The sensation and appearance of this is separation of the "soul" body, or energy body from the physical, like a hand slipping out of a glove. This soul body—now a disembodied aura—then can travel where it pleases, inhibited only by the conscious mind's own limits

168

of acceptance, and can perceive its surroundings wherever it may be, just as though it had its physical sensory organs along. There is a distinct sensation of motion as it proceeds to other locales, and this wandering energy body remains connected to the inert physical body at all times by a tenuous, infinitely extensible thread—the classical "silver cord," surrounded by a haze of the person's normal conscious-level aura. Other than the cord, that aura is absent about the physical body, which is now functioning at a greatly reduced metabolic level resembling suspended animation. Although I normally don't perceive auras, I can readily tell when Marianne is out of body by the somewhat alarming reductions in her level of breathing, muscle tone, and radiant body temperature in contrast to her normal sleeping state. Her reentry is marked by an abrupt jolt or shudder and resumption of normal metabolic activity. Information she may bring back from one of these excursions comes by way of her direct, conscious-level perception, which has somehow been separated from her physical body and transported to the actual locale of those perceptions. This is not clairvoyance.

While science quite understandably refuses to accept that a conscious mind can see without physical eyes or hear without physical ears, those who experience the out-of-body state are certain that it can. This seems to be corroborated by some individuals who, having experienced the out-of-body state of a near-death experience during surgery, shock their doctors with accurate details of devices and occurrences in the operating room that were out of sight to their physical eyes even had they been open and aware. From this and Marianne's experience, we conclude that the conscious mind, when free of the body, can perceive without physical sensory organs. Then it seems entirely reasonable and likely that the Superconscious similarly can perceive its surroundings (physical *and* astral) with equal facility. It is, we believe, those perceptions that the SC chooses to impart, and the conscious-mind receptivity of the individual to detect and interpret them, that distinguishes clairvoyantly acquired knowledge from that obtained through conscious-mind astral travel.

The perceptions in clairvoyance usually are of contemporary events; a sort of "live psychic TV." But, as we have seen before, time in nonphysical realms is indeterminant, if not nonexistent, so metaphysics also deals strongly in perceptions of the past and possible future. One of the psychic talents commonly taken to reveal past events is *psychometry*. Stereotypically, the psychometrist can grasp a subject's long-used personal object—a ring, wallet, item of apparel—and receive, ostensibly from it, impressions concerning the individual's past. These may involve such details as family and romantic relationships; deeds committed with intense emotion, including murder; other major incidents in the subject's past; and perhaps even present whereabouts or circumstances.

A variation of this talent was exemplified by psychic Peter Hurkos when he assisted police investigators seeking criminals. Given a photograph of, say, a murder victim or the location where the body was found, he often was able to receive impressions of the circumstances leading to the violence, and images of the perpetrators. And he would do so while the photograph still was sealed in its opaque envelope. The photographs were not personal relics of the victims, of course, but this is psychometry, nevertheless. There can be no question that it does work for those who do have the gift of psychometric sensitivity.

A conventional explanation for this ability to obtain psychic impressions from personal belongings is that the material object has absorbed the "vibrations" of the owner's unique individuality and is a miniature recording of all that the owner has experienced (during possession of the object, at least). The psychometrist may actually experience some sort of tingle, warmth, vibration, or other sensation of energy upon contact with the object. This concept of perceptible but scientifically unverifiable "vibrations" is used to explain countless psychic states and perceptions, including such things as endowing water with benevolent energies through blessing it as holy water, wearing gem stones having "vibrations" compatible with or complementary to your own, the emanations of planets influencing our astrological circumstances, the various "vibrational levels" that distinguish differing astral states, etc. Are there really such vibrations?

As I have pointed out throughout this book, subjective perceptions frequently are not supported by physical realities. It's also a bit difficult to formu-

171

late to my satisfaction a mechanism whereby inorganic solids, such as jewelry and other personal items, can "absorb" and retain one's personality and memory patterns as the psychometrists believe.

If you believe that holding an object is necessary for revealing information; if your mind tells you that you're feeling vibrations and perceiving some inanimate record embedded in subtle energy matrices surging within the object, then this is the ritual through which you can most effectively tune to pertinent input from your SC. You may find yourself unable to discern such psychic knowledge without contacting an object only because, on the conscious level, you *believe* it to be the source and therefore you disbelieve that the knowledge is perceivable to you without that contact. This sort of conscious-level disbelief closes many doors to psychic knowledge, and is a major reason I urge you to avoid blind acceptance of many "conventional" explanations of metaphysical mechanisms.

The more flexible and open you keep your belief structure, the less you limit your personal reality to erroneous metaphysical concepts, or even to merely incomplete ones. Psychometry is a case in point.

Practitioners from wizards to witch doctors have their different physical objects to "read," among the more usual of which are the witch doctor's entrails of a sacrificed animal, the gypsy's tea leaves, and the wizard's crystal ball. In these, the nonsensitive observer sees only what is physically there: entrails or tea leaves in helter-skelter disarray or a clear glass ball reflecting only its physical surroundings. But the psychic using one of these objects for a focal point of personal attunement "sees"—perceives—patterns, symbols, or literal images that are projected into the conscious mind by the psychic's Superconscious.

These perceptions can be very real to the psychic. The entrails, leaves, and crystal ball really are nothing more than a focal screen to project images into the conscious perception.

A related talent for seeing things that aren't there is *aura perception*. This usually is explained as an uncommon ability to perceive an energy field that is radiated by the human body (or all living things, or all material things, depending on who is doing the explaining). This mysterious field has thus far defied detection and explanation in terms of known physical energies, so each metaphysician is free to describe it in his own terms. Perhaps the most common concept is that it is some form of "psychic" energy; others believe it is a "life force," the "etheric body," *prana*, "orgone energy," or any of several other names for presumed but unprovable emanations or "vibrations" that are perceivable by some persons but invisible to most of us.[3]

It is interesting—and a little confusing—to learn

---

[3]Kirlian photography, a method of photographing what appear to be radiations from finger tips and other living objects, is touted by some as physical proof of the emanation of auric energy. In fact, the technique utilizes externally applied electrical fields and it appears that the energy producing the photographic exposures is *corona discharge*, a well-known electrical phenomenon. The evidence indicates that the intensity and coloring of these discharges are indeed *influenced* by the living organism—its state of health, emotional intensity, etc.—but it seems erroneous to claim that the Kirlian photographs are literal images of the "auric field."

173

that two percipients of auras may see quite different manifestations around the same visual target. For instance, one may see a narrow band of blue thinly outlining only a person's head, while the other may see about that same person a brilliant yellow emanation radiating about and away from the entire body to a radius of a foot or more. Are these two psychics perceiving the same thing? Or is it possible that the traditional concept of aura energy is wrong?

It is terribly risky in metaphysics to positively assert that *anything* is or is not possible. Certainly there are many known radiations from the countless electrical, chemical, and thermal processes continuously transpiring in the body, and it seems likely that others will come to light as science slowly progresses along the frontiers of knowledge. And it may indeed be that some sensitives can detect one or another of these actual energies as the classical explanation of aura perception assumes. But my own observations convince me that there is an explanation for aura perception, at least as practiced by some psychics, that doesn't require a "real" energy field about the target.

What *can* account for it, you must have guessed by now, is the Superconscious. What a psychic perceives as auras about a person can be projections—like those in the crystal ball—from the SC, rather than perceptions of literal energy fields existing in three-dimensional space and time. According to Astar, Cayce, and other proponents of the concept of the superconscious mind, it has the ability to discern the personality characteristics and

174

emotional states of another person through paranormal channels, so the auras it projects into the perceptions of the psychic can in fact be consistently valid. *And they can as easily be projected into the mind's eye for photos and drawings as for live individuals.*

Perhaps closely related to perception of auras surrounding mortals is perception of auras or apparitions of disembodied entities. This covers a broad spectrum ranging from what we think of here as the "soul" aura, which is the conscious-level aura seen to leave the body during an out-of-body experience or to temporarily hover about it following death; the Spirit aura, which is the superconscious-level entity observed either apart from or merged into its associated mortal, and into which the "soul" aura may be seen to merge at some interval following death; and various categories of discarnate entities that reside in specific locations, some of whom fall into the category of ghosts.[4]

It apparently is possible upon occasion for a discarnate entity to draw physical energy into a sufficiently dense pattern to be seen by ordinary optical eyesight. With a manifestation of this type appearing in a room containing several people, it would be possible for everyone present (and presumably a camera) to perceive the entity. It is far more

---

[4]Our experiences include a few with entities that can only be called ghosts. Ghosts and apparitions fall into several classifications, the detailing of which is beyond the scope of this chapter and our limited experience. Metaphysical literature is rife with anecdotal and researched ghost lore and hypotheses; if you find the subject of great interest, I suggest you sample some of the prolific writings of ghost chaser Hans Holzer as a starting point.

usual, though, for only one or two among a number of persons to perceive the presence of a discarnate entity; others, even upon being prompted, will fail to detect anything uncommon. These percipients are sensitives, of course, which simply means their Superconsciouses choose to project into their conscious minds the presence and locations of such visiting entities.

The question then naturally occurs: are there actually discarnate entities present, or is the sensitive's SC simply projecting imaginary images for some obscure purpose? Of course the latter is possible, but we understand that, in most instances, the SC is simply allowing the mortal to perceive the presence of other distinct entities. The detail in which they are shown varies greatly, ranging from mere "blobs" of luminescence in vaguely human proportions to highly detailed images including details of dress and accessories.[5] When such detail is given, it seems to be with the intent to firmly indentify the individual present, or to identify the era or geographical locale with which the individual was associated during its favorite or most fruitful mortal lifetime. As with most metaphysical realities, there is great variety and inconsistency of structure and protocol among discarnate manifesta-

---

[5] It's interesting that even though clothing is a product of physical reality, entities of the nonphysical realms nevertheless usually respect our sensibilities by presenting themselves to our perception in some type of attire. Too, apparitions of departed ones who suffered ravages of disease or injury often appear to their bereaved as whole, hearty, and at their favorite age. It seems that one's personal reality in nonphysical realms can be whatever one thinks it to be; at least the projected images of it can be.

tions. But they do exist, at least within the reality structures of those who perceive them, even though orthodox science can't accommodate them in the scientific paradigm.

Another category of metaphysics could be called *interpretation of ordered structures*. This differs from interpretation of random structures such as tea leaves, animal entrails, smoke patterns, and numerous other things used as focal objects to catalyze intuitive insights. Ordered structures include the charts of astrology, sticks of *I Ching*, cards of Tarot, rune stones adorned with Celtic symbols, lines of the palm of the hand, etc. The techniques of "reading" these often are taught as merely the interpretation of ordered structures on an intellectual level, but in fact there must be psychic insights involved if the information is to have high validity.

The most visible of these is *astrology*, which persists in attracting a large and loyal following despite the oft-expressed outrage of the scientific community over a society that persists in this enlightened age to pay homage to such "superstitions." After all, it does seem irrational to suppose that the physical positions of the sun, moon, and the planets at the moment of one's birth could have the minutest smidgen of influence on one's personality and the course of one's life. Particularly the planets, multiple millions of miles distant. True, we do know the moon influences the tides and the sun controls our climate, but the distant planets guide our lives? Nonsense! And the constellations—star groupings at inconceivable distances? Even more preposterous, particularly in light of the fact that the constellations today actually are not where the astrological charts place them, because our orbit around the galaxy has caused the constellations to shift in our skies during the centuries since astrology was born in Mesopotamia.

I have to agree with all the above, excepting for one small problem: I have seen the uncannily accurate information that comes with high consistency from properly prepared and interpreted astrological data. And in keeping with the criteria I set forth earlier in this book, I accept astrology by a gifted practitioner as valid personal reality because it *works*. I don't have to know how, interesting though that might be.[6]

It doesn't work well at the superficial level, however. The popular newspaper columns deal only with sun signs, which take into account only one of the several heavenly bodies whose positions contribute as indicators of personality and life activities, so they perforce are uselessly general. Persons born on the same month and day but in different years will ordinarily have greatly diver-

---

[6] I doubt that the distant planets have any mysterious emanations that somehow subtly influence individual lives here. However, since everything in nature operates in cycles, I can envision some sort of synchronicity between human life cycles and the celestial cycles, so that the positions of the planets may relate to the points of the life cycles into which we were born, much as the position of the hands of a clock relate to the earth's diurnal cycle only because they move in synchronicity with it; they don't *cause* it. Nevertheless, the hands on the clock are valid for predicting the coming of darkness, the onset of hunger pangs, and countless other details of daily activity that are not caused by the clock but can be accurately inferred from it.

gent horoscopes, as will those born on the same day of the same year but in different geographical locations or even in the same place but at widely different times of the day. Not only the date of birth, but the time—preferably to the minute—and the geographical location are required for developing a useful horoscope. Because few persons go this deeply into astrology, they are disenchanted by its apparent failure. Only when you study the subject in depth can you judge it fairly. More than one writer has undertaken an investigation of astrology with the intention of discrediting it into oblivion, only to find upon deeper research that it does in fact work and is worthy of positive exposition rather than ridicule.

But valid interpretations don't come from superficial astrological knowledge. Marianne spent six months of weekends in intensive study under expert Wes Hubbard to master astrology and Tarot, and I have had the opportunity to observe the effort she takes in working up an individual's chart, from which I have concluded that *I* will never invest the study necessary to become conversant in the subject. But I've also had numerous opportunities to observe and evaluate the validity of information she infers from her astrological charting and interpretations for a considerable variety of subjects, and I brook no doubts that her readings usually have a high degree of validity. In the hands of a qualified practitioner and psychic, astrology works. So *there*, Mr. Skeptic!

But if the information to be gleaned from astrological relationships is based on data so specific and physical as the positions of heavenly bodies at given times, what role does psychic intuition play? Even some astrologers believe they're practicing an exact science; can't a computer perform the same function as an astrologer? In fact, aren't some astrologers now using computers in their work?

These are perfectly reasonable questions. In truth, the computer is a useful tool to the astrologer, saving much of the tedious effort of looking up tables and making calculations of planetary positions for plotting a chart. Once an accurate astrological program is loaded into a computer, obtaining a printed tabulation or even a graphic chart of the pertinent positions for any given birthdate, time, and location is a simple matter of a few keystrokes. It is possible even to load the program with precomposed paragraphs individually relating each of the celestial positions to character traits and potential obstacles and rewards along the life path of the subject. In fact, a chart and appropriate "canned" print-outs are what you are most likely to receive when you mail-order your "personal" horoscope offered for ten dollars or less; a truly individual horoscope, including a chart (which acceptably may be computer generated) and genuine psychic insight into your personal astrological relationships, usually requires more time and effort by a professional astrologer than ten dollars can justify in today's economy.

What makes a valid horoscope is guided *interpretation*. A chart only shows the astrological relationships of sun, moon, planets, and a dozen "houses." And while the major effect of a single body at a given position in one "house"—say, Mars in Capricorn—can be simply expressed in a brief statement, all the other bodies and their locations act to modify that isolated effect, sometimes drastically, and it is to determine the overall effects of all these variables interacting with each other that requires interpretation by the intuitive or psychic capabilities of a human mind. Today's computers can't analyze multiple nonspecific and simultaneously interactive elements, and neither can scientific logic. It requires that peculiar ability of the human mind to arrive at valid conclusions without linear logic to obtain a "feel" for the answer.

Since two dozen variables interacting simultaneously can produce a virtual infinity of possible patterns, the uniqueness of an individual's astrological "influences" can't be accurately defined by guesswork. This is where the astrologer's psychic ability must come into play if the horoscope is to most accurately describe its subject. Only with information gleaned by the astrologer's Superconscious from the SC of the subject can maximum validity of the astrological reading be obtained. So says Astar, and our experience leads us to agree with him in this instance. The computer calculations, the tabulated positions of the planets, the chart—all are only a skeletal structure, which must be fleshed out in detail and meaning by intuitive input from the astrologer's higher self gained through its access to information from the subject's higher self. Psychic insight is a vital element of valid astrological interpretation.[7]

Interpretation of naturally existing ordered structures, such as the planetary positions, permits no question of the psychic's influence in creating those structures: there is none. The question of influence is not so easily answered, however, for the great number of psychic techniques wherein the practitioner plays some part in the creation or manipulation of the structures or objects used as interpretive tools. A prime case in point is the "reading" of Tarot cards.

Tarot cards are the ancestor of today's playing cards used for poker, bridge, and practically all modern card games. In fact, some psychics "read" from ordinary playing cards, but one or another of the several versions of the Tarot deck is preferred by most serious card-reading psychics.

A standard Tarot deck contains seventy-eight cards, arranged in four suits of thirteen cards each plus twenty-six Major Aracana cards (it is the Major Arcana cards that provide fine points of interpretation and emphasis to a reading). Along with suit and rank identification, each face card—and in most decks, each numbered card—is imprinted with a unique picture rife with symbolism. Different sets of illustrations were developed by various devoted

---

[7]This is one reason why scientists who have seriously tried to find agreement between personality traits indicated by the formal structures of astrology and those of test subjects have failed to find convincing validity of the discipline. Most are not tuned to intuitive interpretation, and wouldn't accept its validity if they were. There is practically nothing logical about astrology, but—in the right hands—there is much that is valid.

Tarot practitioners of the past; one that remains popular today is the Thoth deck, attributed to Aleister Crowley, a remarkable, highly controversial, and patently unscrupulous metaphysicist of nineteenth-century Europe and England. Its origin notwithstanding, the Crowley deck is widely used today by psychics of all persuasions. Other popular ones are the Waite deck and the Aquarian deck.

As with astrology, proficiency in interpreting Tarot cards requires long study and much practice. The fact that Tarot symbolism has its roots in astrological lore simplifies things for one already versed in astrology; some individuals study the two disciplines in parallel. In both disciplines, interpretation requires evaluating the significance of each element of symbolism within the context of other symbols appearing in the particular reading as they relate to the particular subject.

If astrology appears to be a study of happenstance—the positions the planets happen to be occupying at a given moment and location—Tarot appears to be a study of pure chance; of symbols on cards shuffled and turned up simply at random. Therefore its validity as a meaningful discipline is totally rejected by orthodox science. This attitude is rational, logical, and predictable among men of reason who have not researched it in great depth. And understandable. My own common sense insists that there can be no possible correlation between thoroughly shuffled and dealt cards and the personal characteristics and proclivities of a subject for whom they are ostensibly being read. But there is a major obstacle to my common-sense conclusion: Given a gifted (meaning psychic) practitioner, Tarot *works*! Often to the great astonishment of the subject, who may feel that his/her innermost privacy has somehow been invaded. I can offer no rational excuse for this; no logical mechanism by which the cards that turn up in a reading seem somehow to have been purposefully positioned in the deck such that they will lay out in a spread symbolically representative of the subject of the reading. But I am satisfied that Tarot card reading does defy random chance and produce symbol arrays that can be interpreted to the genuine benefit of the subject.

There are nearly as many techniques for reading Tarot cards as there are Tarot practitioners. Depending on the reader and the type of information sought, a Tarot spread may be as few as four cards or as many as all seventy-eight. Marianne variously uses a four-card spread, a "Celtic Cross" layout, and a fourteen-card variation of the ten-card "Tree of Life" (or "Quaballah," in any of its various spellings) spread. Before dealing, she asks the subject the general nature or scope of information or counsel desired from the reading. Then she thoroughly shuffles the entire deck several times through and asks the subject to cut the deck (usually three times) in any proportions and to restack them into a full deck in any order and orientation he/she chooses. Marianne then deals sequentially from the top of the deck, laying the cards face up in the number and pattern appropriate to the type of spread she has elected to use. Upon examination of the revealed symbols *as they relate to one another* in position within the spread as well as with respect to the information sought, she usually arrives at an interpretation of the reading that—while it may be meaningless to Marianne—usually is understood and deemed pertinent by the subject of the reading.

It is important to stress that this process is not "fortune telling," which seems to be what most persons seek in psychic readings, but is the gaining of insight into the personality traits, emotional forces, and interpersonal activities currently influencing the subject's inner and external realities. From this, the subject can infer the alternative possible personal futures resulting from his/her choice of actions in the present, which allows that subject to better *control* that future, not just foretell it. This is the real value of valid psychic counseling, whatever metaphysical tools the counselor may utilize.

One can argue whether the Superconscious of the subject influences the physical order of the cards before they are dealt, but the role of the Tarot reader's SC in interpreting them after they're dealt is vital. As with an astrological chart, a Tarot spread contains a number of *interactive* symbols that can only be interpreted within the context of the spread as a whole. Moreover, the range of possible meanings for any given Tarot symbol is far broader and more loosely defined than is true of astrological symbols, and interpretation of an array of imprecise but interactive symbols by purely analytical means is impossible. It follows, then, that only the Superconscious of the subject can identify the nuances of symbology appropriate to the individual.

It then can pass them on to the Tarot reader's SC telepathically and, if the reader is psychic (receptive to her/his superconscious input), the Tarot spread can be interpreted with high validity.

Psychic ability notwithstanding, consistently valid Tarot reading doesn't come quickly or easily. Perhaps even more than astrology, Tarot requires intimate familiarization with the spectrum of symbol meanings—there are seventy-eight cards, remember—and the virtually infinite variety of ways in which they can interact with others in the spread. The time and effort required for study and practice, and a mind open to possible psychic input, are two ingredients many scientists are unwilling to devote to an objective examination of Tarot; until they recognize and overcome this unwillingness, they will remain unable to credit its validity.

Whether the physical order of the cards within the deck is subject to psychic manipulation is debatable, but there can be no question that physical manipulation of some sort occurs in the various forms of *dowsing*. The best known of these is sometimes called "water witching," in which the dowser seeks to locate—to "divine"—underground sources of water. Stereotypically, the dowser grasps a forked willow or witch hazel branch, a stem in each hand, and points the central leg of the fork horizontally in front of him as he paces across the ground of interest. A downward dip of the central leg signifies that he has located a site of subterranean water. As is true of most psychic practitioners, each dowser has a unique symbolism code. By the degree to which the fork seems to bend, or the abruptness of its movement, or through other subjective sensations, a dowser may be able to estimate the depth at which water will be found, or to evaluate the quantity (will it supply the demand of a proposed well?), or the quality (is it heavily laden with obnoxious minerals?). But whatever the specifics of its symbolism, the art of dowsing certainly involves physical deflection of a material object. What moves it?

The most logical answer is the dowser's muscles. This is not an accusation of willful manipulation, but an assertion that involuntary muscular movement occurs. The fact is that the fork must be held in human hands for it to respond. Affix it mechanically to the front end of a tractor, and you could drive over the search area all day without a single mysterious bow of the bough. Ergo, the manipulative ingredient in conventional dowsing must be the human holding the branch. Even when the dowser exclaims, "It felt like it was going to pull it right out of my grip," it surely must be his own muscles—and/or some aspect of his psyche—that are contributing to the perception.[8]

Modern dowsers are likely to prefer dowsing

---

[8]Some accounts insist that the divining fork actually *bends* downward at the far end against the dowser's angle of grip. I have not personally observed such a convincing demonstration of "external" forces but, if such accounts are accurate, there must be other influences manifesting in addition to the dowser's own involuntary muscular changes. The forces may bear some similarity of origin to those speculated about in the forthcoming discussion of poltergeist and levitation phenomena. The fact remains that the fork doesn't respond unless it's held by the human; therefore its movements are controlled by some aspect of that human and his ability to perceive at some level the presence of the water or other target.

rods to the traditional sapling fork. These are L-shaped rods, perhaps with tubular handles arranged like bearings, that are held in the hands like two six-guns, their longer ends pointing forward, parallel to the ground and to each other. With the shorter ends very free to rotate in the hands or handles, the slightest tilting of wrists will cause the outer ends to swing apart, or to cross, or perform other movements. The theory is that minute external forces can easily move them; in truth, so can imperceptible arm and wrist movements. Like the fork, dowsing rods don't work unless they are held by an individual.[9]

Despite ridicule by the world of science, on-site field dowsing is widely practiced today in the ongoing search for water, oil, minerals, underground piping and wiring, and practically anything one seeks. For the phenomenon of dowsing isn't limited to water, but is "tunable" to a target of choice. If you're a dowser and you are seeking the route of underground power cables in your yard, the fork or rods won't respond to the water and sewer lines when you cross them, but will "zero in" on the power lines.

There may be an insignificant market for powerline dowsing but, since there is strong commercial interest in both water and oil resources, it's not surprising that some well drilling firms are said to retain (or even to have been established by) dowsers, who may vie with conventional geologists in

---

[9]You can make you own from wire coat hangers. Since many people are successful with their first attempt at dowsing, you might like to make some and try them.

evaluating potentially successful drilling sites. Their avowed talents aren't publicized to a firm's stockholders, but some seem to enjoy a longevity of employment that implies a satisfactory percentage of hits.

A common explanation offered for the mechanism behind field dowsing is that each physical element and compound in existence radiates unique "vibrations," which somehow propagate through perhaps as much as a mile of rock and soil to impinge upon the dowser's "receptors," thereby triggering an involuntary muscular response that causes the fork to tilt downward or the rods to swing. At least one scientist, seeking a physiological explanation, has spent many hours researching the location in the human body of such receptors.[10] He finally concluded that when he shielded both sides of the dowser's torso with aluminum plates at roughly the kidney level, they seemed to interfere with the ability to respond to targets. He deduced therefore that some obscure physical sensory organs, selectively susceptible to the various supposed unique radiations of the target materials, reside in that part of the body. Also inherent in his conclusions is the apparent ability of a mere sheet of aluminum to block radiations that can penetrate great thicknesses of soil, rock, water, ores, etc.

There is at least one major flaw in this theory of the mechanism of dowsing: it can't account for *map* dowsing. Even the good professor concedes this.

---

[10]Reported by Dr. Z. V. Harvalik in the "Consciousness Frontiers" seminar of March 31, 1979, at Northern Virginia Community College, Sterling, VA.

Map dowsing, sometimes called *radiesthesia*, is a technique for locating a desired target by searching a map representing the physical area where the target is sought, instead of pacing the premises in person. The dowsing tool most readily used for this is a pendulum, which may be as simple as a needle suspended by a length of thread or as elaborate as an exotic crystal on the end of a delicate chain of precious metal. It is held in the hand of the dowser and slowly moved about just above the map's surface, accompanied by the dowser's request that it respond to spot(s) on the map corresponding to the location(s) of the target in the actual physical area. This method is used by some psychics for seeking everything from oil deposits to lost persons, with probably as much success as others obtain in actual field dowsing.

Each psychic has his/her own pendulum code. For one individual, the pendulum may swing in a clockwise circle for yes and counterclockwise for no. For another, it may change from a circular motion to a linear back-and-forth motion. Or stop swinging. Or start. The absolute motion doesn't matter, so long as the operator can correctly interpret its symbolism.

A pendulum operator will swear that he or she is holding the supporting hand perfectly still and that the pendulum is moving of its own volition in response to some external energy—but it is clear to an observer that the operator's hand *is* actually moving, ever so slightly, thereby causing the pendulum to respond. Like the dowsing fork on a tractor, a pendulum suspended from a rigid frame will not move when maps of targets are placed below it. It must be held by an operator, whose muscles impart the motion, involuntary though it may be; this seems to eliminate any mysterious external energies at work.

What accounts for the dowser's muscular response to the presence of targets or target symbols? It's certainly not the conscious mind, because the dowser would not be seeking information of which she/he was already aware. So is it the subconscious, as many people contend? Not as we use the term here, where we perceive the subconscious to be little more than an "autopilot" programmed to respond in fixed ways to mundane stimuli, having no sentience and no independent perceptual facility.

We are left, then, with that other aspect of human mind—the one with independent and superphysical perceptual facilities; with independent powers of induction, deduction, and decision; and the power of subtle action through the physical body: the superconscious mind. Just as it can transcend the physical to discern the positions of cards in a deck, the superconscious mind can sense the location of the target and direct the muscular movements causing the fork or pendulum to respond appropriately. (When the target is a missing person or crime victim, telepathy—communication between the SCs of the dowser and target person—may also come into play.) This explanation for the mechanism of dowsing ties the whole phenomenon into a neat, simple package. We don't need any mysterious, uniquely identifying "vibrations" somehow radiating through great depths of soil and rock, and we don't need to scratch our heads over the seeming impossibility of detecting such vibrations from a mere map. Crediting the phenomenon of dowsing to those same powers of the SC that underlie all other psychic phenomena accounts as easily for map dowsing as for on-site dowsing. As I've said several times, there is a great variety of ways in which individuals are sensitive to signals from their respective higher minds; the successful dowser is one whose motor muscles are responsive to subtle input from his/her SC.

Dowsing establishes that the incarnate SC can impart motion to material objects by influencing its mortal's muscles. It takes no great act of faith to accept this; it seems entirely logical that if many muscles are controlled by the subconscious, and many are under conscious, volitional control, and some (such as those for breathing) may be either, then it's not unreasonable to conclude that some also may be responsive to control at the superconscious level. But we must go beyond this, if we are going to explain all paranormal phenomena in terms of the powers of the Superconscious, because there is a great anecdotal body of literature documenting nonphyiscal manipulation of material objects, some of it detailing activities of apparently discarnate entities. Explaining this—in *any* terms— is difficult. But since one person's theory in this area is as good as any other's, I'm game to take a shot at it.

Probably the most publicized manifestations of inexplicable manipulation of material objects are *psychokinesis* (or sometimes *telekinesis*) and *poltergeist* phenomena. The former defines movement of objects through voluntary, willful mental effort alone; the latter is alleged to be involuntary, nonconscious movement of objects without contact, often attributed to a maladjusted, pubescent child residing in the household plagued by "noisy ghost" pranks. These are but two of a rather broad category of "mental" manipulations of physical matter of energy in ways that defy scientific explanation and which therefore are denied by orthodox science.

It is a fundamental law of physics that imparting relative motion to a physical object (mass) requires a force acting on that mass; when that force acts through a physical distance (as in lifting a book from a table to some point above it), work is performed. This is the basic definition of work; further, work can be performed only through the expenditure of energy.[11] The point of this is that, according to our accepted structure of physical reality, moving a material object by "mind" power alone still results in measurable physical work being done and therefore represents a corresponding expenditure of physical energy. Raising a book an inch off a table against the pull of gravity requires a force acting through a distance (*work*, by

---

[11] *Conversion* of energy, actually, such as from the "potential" energy bound in gasoline to the "kinetic" energy—the mass in motion—of a moving automobile. Prior to Einstein, energy was considered to be changeable but indestructible. We now know that in atomic fission and fusion, energy can be converted to matter and vice versa, but conservation of energy still holds for all ordinary physical processes.

definition), and the "potential" energy of that book (a very real and recoverable energy) is increased by exactly the amount of energy spent in lifting it. Where does this energy come from when, say, a "poltergeist" raises a book from a table and sails it across the room? Is it some "psychic" energy that escapes the instruments of science? Strong enough to move a book of several pounds but undetectable by instruments that can measure forces in millionths of a pound? Or are the scientists simply not in the right place at the right time?

The energy behind the "conventional" poltergeist phenomenon, in which very material objects are moved about, often violently, is commonly alleged to be supplied by the disturbed youth typically associated with the afflicted household (although not all poltergeist sites have a resident youth). In some fashion, so the theory goes, the budding adolescent is able to subconsciously, albeit unknowingly, project energy to manipulate objects at a distance. This poses a question: if a person is supplying this very real energy from his/her own physical resources—even though it's done subconsciously— why isn't he/she exhausted by the effort? And how can it be that poltergeist pranks sometimes include moving objects heavier than one person could manipulate directly?

And it's not only poltergeists that mysteriously command physical energies. For instance, there was Saint Joseph, of Cupertino, Italy, who became a Franciscan monk in 1625. He proved to be exceedingly pious, given to attaining highly ecstatic states during worship services. It seems well attested to that he frequently was seen by fellow monks and assembled congregations to literally rise from the floor and float in the air in moments of high ecstasy. In fact, it allegedy is on record that he ultimately was expelled from the choir because his " . . . noisy levitations disturbed his fellow friars."[12] On one memorable occasion, he is said to have been in a far corner of the chapel to pray by himself, when he suddenly uttered a cry, levitated above the congregation, and "flew" to the altar; he then emitted another cry and sailed back over the assemblage to his prayer corner and settled to the floor. These rather startling incidents naturally attracted considerable notice and investigation, including that of the German philosopher Leibnitz, who personally observed some of the monk's levitations and believed them to be genuine.

The fascinating aspect of this is that his levitation apparently was involuntary and consciously uncontrollable, and the hapless monk was greatly embarrassed by the suspicion and disapproval his antics drew from his superiors. Nevertheless, their investigations found no evidence of trickery, and Joseph of Cupertino eventually was appointed by the church to sainthood.

Then there was Daniel Dunglas Home, a nineteenth-century metaphysicist of worldwide fame—or infamy, depending on who's telling it. Born in Scotland and reared largely in the United States, he came to prominence in England and on the Con-

---

[12]*Mysterious Powers.* London: Aldus Books Limited, 1975.

tinent by lecturing and demonstrating great talent in many areas of metaphysics. Frequently included in his repertoire was the act of rising perpendicularly from the floor, his arms above his head, and hovering in midair for five minutes or so before easing back to the floor. Upon one occasion, he startled a gathering of gentlemen on the third floor of a clubhouse by excusing himself and leaving the room, only to appear moments later *outside* a window of the room he had just left, hovering vertically and tapping on the glass for attention. His explanation was that he had gone down the hall, exited through an open window, and levitated alongside the building to the window where he was seen. Upon being asked to demonstrate, he led the gentlemen through the hall to a window that was open only about a foot. One of the members expressed some doubt that a man could exit through an opening of that size, whereupon Home proceeded to go through it headfirst, in a face-up, horizontal position. He exited fully and then, moments later, reemerged feet first, as though he had merely floated out into the night on his back and then, without changing position, reversed direction and floated back in. All of this occurring three floors above a London street! An observer's written account of this demonstration concedes that the darkness of the night conceivably could have concealed props or devices used by Home, but he was at a loss to explain how they could have been rigged and used.

Before Uri Geller's emergence a few years ago, D. D. Home was perhaps the most-investigated practitioner in the history of metaphysics. He underwent rigorous testing on both sides of the Atlantic, including investigation by the respected scientist Sir William Crookes. In addition to his prestigious accomplishments and positions in English science, Crookes was once president of the British Society for Psychical Research, and he is on record as having never caught Home in trickery or fraud.[13] And if it's true that Home regularly levitated in front of lecture audiences, then perhaps floating unsupported high above a street is only a more daring exhibition of a genuine power. On the other side of the world it has long been alleged that some eastern mystics, usually after prolonged exercise of great physical and mental discipline, develop the ability to levitate themselves at will. Thousands of eyewitness reports of levitating mystics have been brought back to the western world, and still photos alleging to show this have been widely published; yet few of us can say from direct personal knowledge that such things are possible, so the debunkers still hold sway over public belief.

Soviet scientists, some of whom apparently take their metaphysical research more seriously than do most of ours, have conducted extensive experiments in telekinesis, and certain subjects apparently have been able, in the laboratory, to move small objects purely by mental effort. Perhaps the most noted is Nelya Mikhailova, also known as Madame Kulagina. Apparently she is able to move very small articles—matchsticks, pencils, etc.—

---

[13] *Spirits and Spirit Worlds.* London: Aldus Books Limited, 1975.

197

without touching them.[14] Motion pictures of her psychokinetic activities have—predictably—been labeled by our own emotionally committed skeptics as fraudulent, while testing of her abilities in the US has been labeled inadequately controlled.

It's interesting that Mikhailova requires intense concentration to move very light objects about on a level surface, and is exhausted after a laboratory session. This suggests that she uses much *more* physical energy than is required to perform the actual work, while levitation (and poltergeist activity) seems to use much less. Perhaps *tele*kinesis by conscious-mind power is a roundabout, inefficient method, while *psycho*kinesis performed at some other level of consciousness is more direct. Maybe the two words could be assigned different meanings accordingly.

While I can't prove it, I presently believe that telekinesis and/or psychokinesis is possible, so I can accept the Soviet claims at face value until they're proven otherwise. I also suspect that bodily levitation is possible. After all, if a poltergeist can move heavy furnishings by some level of consciousness, surely one's own body can be raised and moved as well.

But where does the energy come from? Remember that—by definition—there is real, physical-energy expenditure involved. More, it would seem in some cases, than is available from the physical body. To get around this objection, metaphysicists

---

[14] Sheila Ostrander and Lynn Schroeder, in *Psychic Discoveries Behind the Iron Curtain*, Englewood Cliffs, N.J.: Prentice-Hall, Inc., 1970

proclaim the existence of "psychic" energy. This is a mysterious energy that is thus far undetectable by physical science and yet is credited with forcefully influencing physical objects, some of them of considerable weight. Ostensibly a nonphysical consciousness, be it subconscious, superconscious, or "ghost," possesses or has at its command a substantial degree of psychic energy, perhaps in the form of nonphysical "muscles."

Alternatively, the universe is believed by some to be saturated with an unlimited supply of "psychic" or universal energy that can be manipulated by consciousnesses that learn how. This is perceived to be a "neutral," nondirected energy; like electricity, it can be used for good or ill, depending entirely on the person using it. This neatly sidesteps the question of how an individual can expend more than his own energy: he doesn't need to supply it; all he needs is to *control* it. Just as you don't supply the motive power for your car; you simply control—with very little physical effort—the energy residing in gasoline to make it go.

The various concepts of psychic energy are invoked to explain a broad spectrum of paranormal phenomena, from the astrological "vibrations" of the planets to the "kundalini" forces ascribed to the human glandular centers. Here, as in all aspects of metaphysics, there is little accord among practitioners as to the actual nature of such energy. Or even as to its existence.

This opens the door for me to propose a mechanism through which known physical energies and objects may be influenced by conscious or superconscious direction—through influencing real vibrations. So far as I know, no other metaphysicist has ever broached this postulate: *the superconscious mind can invalidate the natural laws of chance.* It can do so by injecting a bias into the otherwise random vibrations at the molecular and/or atomic levels of physical reality. In its essence, this concept may explain how an entity—mortal or astral—can interact with material objects in ways ranging from levitation to spirit photography.

I described earlier (in Chapter 2) how a seemingly solid physical object is known to actually be composed of countless atoms separated by relatively vast spaces, forming molecules that are vibrating in random directions and with energies dependent on the object's temperature (actually the temperature is a measure of the molecular vibrational energy). So a "solid" body really is made up of millions or billions of separate particles of matter, each one vibrating in its own little volume of space. Various internal forces of attraction and repulsion interact to keep the body from flying apart (as indeed it does, when in a free gaseous state). But why does it ordinarily remain stationary overall? Why don't all of the particles happen once in a while to move all the same way at the same instant, making the whole physical body move spontaneously?

The answer lies in the natural law of averages. At any given instant, there is some number of particles that are all moving leftward in their vibration, but there also are approximately as many moving rightward at that same instant. Thus the forces in the two directions are balanced and the object does not move.

Further, because the elastic binding forces in a solid are strong, the particles tending to move away from the surface are pulled back to it and the object remains intact as well as stationary.[15]

We have shown how opposing directions of particle vibration balance each other. Bear in mind that there always are particles moving in every conceivable direction, with about the same number moving in exactly the opposite direction at the same instant, so the physical object remains stationary. This is because the laws of average and chance dictate that in a volume constraining a large number of randomly moving (and colliding) identical bodies, there will be about equal numbers moving in every direction at any and every instant. The greater the number of bodies, the closer those numbers approach exact equality. Thus for any practical physical object, with its millions or billions of particles, the probability that all the random motions will average out to perfect equilibrium approaches mathematical certainty. The statistical likelihood of a significantly disproportionate number of particles moving the same direction simultaneously—which would produce a force tending to move the object—is vanishingly small. *Maybe* once every few million or billion years.

Suppose, now, that some level of mind has the ability to inject its influence (perhaps by directing psychic or astral "energy") into that body and to somehow "unbalance" the laws of chance. It may

---

[15] Most surface molecules are pulled back. In the case of a volatile liquid, however, some surface molecules do break free of the attractive forces and the liquid is said to evaporate.

be that no real energy is required merely to deflect the direction of vibrating particles at the molecular or atomic level, so that effort by some level of consciousness could tilt the numbers from fifty-fifty to, say fifty-five–forty-five in some direction, in which event the body would tend to move in "fifty-five–percent" direction. This ten percent imbalance of internal forces might be sufficient to make a pencil roll on a smooth table, or a pivoted needle to deflect. A much greater vibrational imbalance would be required to raise a human body against the force of gravity; however, the molecules of the body are very intimately linked to the mind and it seems reasonable that their random movements are more readily subject to manipulation by it, so this concept of influencing vibrations conceivably could account for self-levitation as well. If there's anything to the alleged power of mind over matter, it surely must be most applicable to the bodily matter belonging to that mind exercising the power.[16]

The concept of "psychic power" as an ability to override the laws of chance gains some credence from the laboratory. For two hundred years now, we have been testing psychics, metaphysicists, magicians, spiritualists, and mediums in attempts to

---

[16]Conventional energy conservation rules still apply. If a body is raised against the force of gravity, its potential energy is increased. If this energy is not provided by an outside force (such as an elevator), it must be converted from other energies within the body. In this case, it is not muscular energy and measurably not brain energy. Perhaps the temperature energy of the body is lowered? And recovered upon return of the body to its original level? In this connection, it is interesting that alleged *apports*—objects that seem to be suddenly materialized, or *teleported* from elsewhere, often are described as being very cold upon their arrival.

establish some scientific bases for their alleged powers. In general, science hasn't accepted many of the results because they can't be replicated at will under laboratory conditions. But what has come out, from the Rhine's card-guessing experiments at Duke University in the thirties to the latest research into mental influence on random electron behavior is a statistical *deviation from the laws of averages* achieved by some subjects. Rightly "guessing" cards only slightly better than chance allows, or influencing mechanically thrown dice to fall less randomly than they "should," are not impressive to the skeptic, nor reliably useful to the experimenter; they're not predictable and clearcut—but they *are* pretty consistent violations of the laws of chance. And if we truly can override the laws of chance, and learn to control that ability, we can demonstrate many phenomena that science, believing its laws immutable, cannot explain and therefore will not accept. If further it should be true that the randomness of particulate motion can be disturbed—"derandomized"—by mind without injecting physical force, then we don't have to fabricate some mysterious "psychic" energy to account for the physical occurrences accompanying many psychic manifestations.

After all, if consciousness can penetrate and influence vibrational matter at the molecular and/or atomic level, it can influence the state of silver salts in an unexposed photographic film, perhaps producing actual "mind photographs," as Ted Serios is believed by many to be able to do. Or "spirit" photographs, where one long deceased turns up visible in a snapshot, to the astonishment of the photographer. Or, as I noted above, apparently consciousness can influence the distribution of individual electrons in laboratory experiments—a feat no doubt extendable to inducing malfunctions in computers!

I'll touch here on just one more type of matter manipulation by nonphysical means: *electronic voice phenomena*. This is an area that has long interested me, but in which I've only recently begun to study and experiment. It's more popularly called the "Spirit voice" phenomenon, and it involves capturing mysterious voices on audio tape recorders. Since tape recorders have been readily available only since the late 1940s, this facet of metaphysical manifestation is relatively new.

Evidently the pioneer in seeking anomalous voices on tape was Friedrich Jürgenson, a writer and film producer living at the time in Sweden. In 1959, he heard what he believed to be the voice of his deceased mother addressing him as he played back a tape he had just recorded. Years of experimentation following this led in 1964 to his book, *Voices from Space*, a copy of which fell into the hands of Konstantin Raudive, a Latvian-born psychologist practicing in Germany. Raudive undertook his own intensive experimentation, and twenty thousand voices later published *Breakthrough*.[17] Evidently this has become the definitive reference on such phenomena, which often are referred to as "Raudive voices." The book contains testimonials by a num-

---

[17] English translation published by Lancer Books, Inc.; New York, 1971.

ber of highly reputable and learned participators and witnesses attesting to the reality of anomalous voices; even though many of them are too faint to stand out clearly above the inherent noise on the tape, the testimony leaves little doubt that they exist.

The technique for recording these disembodied voices has several variations. The simplest is to simply record with an open microphone, with which you can ask a question and wait in silence for a minute or so. Listening intently upon playback, you *might* hear what sounds like an answer, even though your ears heard nothing during the recording. Raudive and others supposed that the Spirits of the deceased were somehow transmitting radiolike energy from their dimension of existence, so he also used a radio tuned to an ostensibly unused channel for a recording source. (There practically is no such thing as an unused channel. Virtually all radio frequencies are in use with regularity *somewhere* in the world, which means that freak reception, even if only momentary, is possible on a channel that seems locally vacant.) Alternatively, Raudive used a device made for him by a radio technician, which he called a "diode." In fact, it contained a tuned circuit and a diode, and used a short probe for an antenna. In essence, this was what used to be called a "crystal receiver," receptive to a wide range of signal frequencies but having rather poor sensitivity. Again, freak conditions can result in reception by the "diode" box of mundane radio transmissions.

Even when using the microphone, which one would expect to pick up only acoustic signals, it is readily possible for radio signals to penetrate the recorder circuits with sufficient strength to manifest as audio signals on the tape. Many persons have been mystified, upon recording something via microphone, to discover a local station's program mixed with the desired sounds in playback. Or a powerful citizens'-band operator in the neighborhood, or chatter from a passing police cruiser. Radio signals (including TV frequencies) have a knack for intruding where they're not intended to go, sometimes proving nearly impossible to shield from or filter out of a particular electronic device. So we can't absolutely rule out sporadic radio interference as a source of mysterious voices on tape, unless the content of their message is something so clearly directed to the experimenter that no radio transmission could coincidentally contain such material.

Other sources of unexpected sounds on magnetic tape include residual signals due to incomplete erasure of a previous recording, and *print-through*, the slight magnetization of a layer of tape with the pattern recorded on the layer wrapped adjacent to it on the reel or in the cassette. Incomplete erasure usually can be identified if you are familiar with what was previously on the tape; print-through is nearly always present to some degree but is readily identified because it is a faint and muffled replica of the currently playing sound or word, occurring as a "pre-echo" one reel revolution before it, and/or a post-echo one reel revolution after it.

Not only must we be careful to not ascribe sounds from interference, incomplete erasure, and print-through to paranormal sources; we have to be aware of possible tricks played by the listener's mind. The literature on electronic voice phenomena reiterates that most of the anomalous voices are very faint, requiring repeated playing and intense aural concentration to understand them. In communications vernacular, they are "down in the noise" of the tape itself. When I first read of "spirit voice" phenomena, I was reminded of an earlier experience of hearing nonexistent sounds within random noise: after working a shift in a radio broadcast transmitter plant with the program monitor speaker in continuous operation, I would experience a strange aural illusion after sign off: I kept hearing music. The transmitter was cooled by internal blowers, which continued to operate for several minutes after shutdown to dissipate residual heat in the equipment. As I busied myself completing logs and other sign-off details, I seemed to hear music mixed in with the rushing whir of the blowers. I could never quite identify it, and I certainly couldn't account for it, because all the program and monitoring equipment was completely turned off. But when the blowers stopped, the "music" stopped, too. I finally chalked the mystery up to tricks being played on me by ears and mind that had been hearing music in that environment all day, and I arrived at a theory to explain it.

Random noise that has equal energy per "cycle" throughout the audible spectrum is called "white" noise. The whir of fans, the receiver noise between stations on an unmuted, FM radio, and the background hiss of recording tape all resemble white noise in the respect that these sounds are comprised

207

of random impulses whose components spread over most of the audible spectrum. While the hiss of "static" and live electronic equipment sounds like it is only high frequencies, it is easy to demonstrate that there also are components present down through the deepest of bass frequencies.

So what was happening with the blowers? Actually, it's simple: their whir contained random sounds of all frequencies; it was my *mind* that at any given instant was selectively emphasizing my perception of some frequencies and discriminating against others, time-varying the pitch of its emphasis so that melodylike patterns were formed from elements of the noise. In other words, my mind was creating some degree of order out of chaos; by subjectively emphasizing selected frequencies from all those present in the general noise, it was *overriding the laws of chance* as they apply to probabilities of random distribution. Since the "music" consisted of only portions of the total noise, it never could rise above it in loudness but was of necessity buried within it.[18]

Having experienced this perceptual illusion decades ago, I was inclined to dismiss the "spirit

---

[18] If you'd like to try an experiment in the power of suggestion, locate a spot on your FM radio where you're sure no station can be heard (if you have interstation muting, turn it off so that the receiver hiss can be heard); then call in a friend and imply that you need help in identifying or defining a distant station that you can't quite hear clearly enough to understand. Suggest that your friend listen very intently; that his/her excellent hearing ability may be able to catch something you're missing. If you play it right, the chances are very good that your friend will so convincingly "hear" voices or music buried in the noise that he/she will tend to reject your subsequent revelation of the fact that there really was no signal there at all.

208

voices" claimed to exist within tape's inherent hiss as nothing more tangible than the "music" I heard in the transmitter blowers. Except for one obstacle: the taped-voice phenomena are repeatable. The reports of many observers and experimenters leave little doubt that a given "spirit voice" word or phrase occurs at a specific place on the tape and can be repeated by rewinding the tape and playing that spot again. In fact, relistening several times is often required before a word can be understood. On the other hand, there are instances in which multiple participants in a given experiment agreed as to the words they perceived upon their first hearing. Repeatability and agreement among observers are not likely characteristics of a purely subjective, illusory perception, which would bear no fixed, repetitive relationship between the message and actual tape position, and no agreement between individual participants. So I couldn't totally explain away electronic voice phenomena as perceptual illusion. Too many persons insisted that there is something there.

Other experimenters have tried playing tapes back at various speeds and in reverse in attempts to decipher some of the garbled anomalous sounds they encounter. When we sift out all the explicable voices—the CB, freak radio reception, print-through, etc.—we are left with a residue of "voices" that seem to be impressed paranormally. Since we don't know *how* they are impressed, we can't say with certainty *when* they are. There is some reason to believe that at least some of the magnetic patterns are created on the tape during playback.

In a broad sense, we can define the mechanism involved. Magnetic tape is coated with a film containing countless magnetizable particles. In the unrecorded state, the minute residual magnetic fields or domains of the individual particles are randomly distributed and have no pattern of orientation. When you play a blank tape, you hear the hiss of random noise that all these minute magnets induce in the playback head as they pass across it. To record a tape, it is passed across the recording head while a current representing the sound passes through the head coils. This causes many of the little magnets in the coating to align in various patterns corresponding to the head current at the instant they pass across it. In this way, the tape recorder creates orderly patterns out of the random magnetic orientation of the unrecorded tape; these patterns then will induce small, corresponding voltages in the play head when the tape is subsequently drawn across it during playback. Because the magnetic orientations induced in the coating tend to remain fixed, the pattern remains until a stronger magnetic influence again scatters the magnetic orientations—that is, erases the tape.

This process of rearranging random characteristics into some order brings us back to my postulate that the mind may be able to override the laws of chance. If consciousness somehow has the ability to enter into and manipulate "real" energy, then it's not necessary to postulate some mysterious "psychic" energy to rearrange magnetic tape domains into detectable and measurable patterns. All we have to invoke is my model, in which mind at some level can override the physical laws of chance, and let that mind utilize minute portions of the known energies available to rearrange the random magnetism of the tape into patterns that are audible upon playback.

Then do Spirits of the deceased directly utilize this relatively new technology of tape recording to attempt communication, or is there an intermediate step involved? The clue seems to lie in *inviting* voices to manifest.

When Jürgenson first announced the discovery of his deceased mother's voice on tape, he seemed to imply that it happened spontaneously; however, he later conceded that he had been actively seeking such a manifestation for a considerable time before he succeeded. Certainly Raudive and other experimenters are inviting manifestations, and in my very limited experiments, I have had some slight success in obtaining recordings from nonmaterial sources when I was consciously seeking them. This is not to say that anomalous voices may never manifest unbidden. Further, I suspect that essentially *all* such manifestations are accomplished through cooperation by the SC of the experimenter (or of a participant) in somehow manipulating the random distribution of magnetic domains on the tape into patterns that may convey communication.

The involvement of the experimenter is strongly suggested by Raudive's results. A man of great linguistic talent, he is conversant in seven or eight languages, including his native Latvian and its

211

older dialects, along with German, English, French, Spanish, Swedish, and Russian, and his "Spirit" voices on tape spoke in all of these languages. This wouldn't be so startling were it not for the fact that frequently a single voice would use words from several of these languages in a single sentence! Often including languages that the deceased individual allegedly manifesting did not speak while alive. This simply doesn't make sense, if one supposes that the discarnate Spirits communicate from their realm only with difficulty and much practice; why would they needlessly complicate their communications by couching them in a babel of languages?

It's tempting to challenge the claim that Raudive's voices are those of discarnate beings by asserting that anyone who understands so many languages could hear in one burst of random sounds a "word" in one language and in a subsequent burst a "word" in another; thus with a lot of imagination and a wide selection of languages to call upon, a sequence of sounds could be interpreted as a polyglot sentence. This assertion is refuted, however, by the substantial number of reputable individuals, many of them also multilingual, who agree that in fact many sentences obtained by Dr. Raudive unquestionably were composed of words in various languages. Evidently there must be some other explanation.

I suggest that it is the experimenter's mind that, at some level, is instrumental in creating electronic voice phenomena. The fact that such phenomena seem to manifest only when they are sought by an experimenter is one clue, and I suggest that the polyglot nature of the phenomena obtained by Dr. Raudive lends weight to the postulate. They are catalyzed (but not necessarily fabricated, as I shall discuss) by his own deeply ingrained multilingual capabilities.

It is our perception that one's superconscious mind can be communicating and manifesting at any time and any place in affairs totally unrelated to the activities of the conscious mind, so that it could be influencing magnetic domains on tape regardless of the experimenter's focus of attention at the moment.

Then if anomalous voices are actually embedded on tape through agency of the experimenter's SC, they can't be voices of the dead, can they?

Well, why not? There's no reason that EVP (electronic voice phenomena) can't be simply another form of mediumship, in which the energy and mind of a living person are utilized as channels to convey communications from discarnate levels of existence. In conventional mediumship, the body, voice, physical energy, and some level of mental function of the mortal medium (who may be non-conscious during the visitation) are used to convey the words and thoughts of another entity (commonly but not necessarily deceased; the SC of a living person may also speak through a medium); yet the message is not the medium's, but that of the manifesting entity. The speech mannerisms and to some extent even the timbre of the voice may change to reflect the external personality. Even though the medium is instrumental to the process, the message content is created by another entity.

Similarly, automatic writing utilizes the physical energy and some level of the receiver's mind to channel communications from a visiting entity; even the handwriting may take on the characteristics of the manifesting personality's script. And the Ouija board, automatic typing, and various other forms of channelling communications from others all utilize the mind and body of the medium, recipient, or experimenter. So just because we conclude that it is the SC of the experimenter that is the instrument by which anomalous voices are recorded on tape doesn't mean that some of the voice personalities can't be from beyond the grave.

The anomalous voices obtained by Jürgenson and all the experimenters to follow him are presumed by most to be those of departed individuals, and the voices often provide confirmatory identifications. However, just as is true of mediumship and other methods of communication with astral entities, there exists the possibility of impostorship, fraud, and simple mischief on the part of those entities.

As a general rule, we are highly skeptical of entities who claim to be—or to have been—someone of great historical prominence (just as we are of the person who believes he was Napoleon in a previous life). First, we understand that some individuals of past prominence have returned in new mortal incarnations[19]; second, we expect most others to have bet-

_____

[19]Our experience indicates that reincarnation by a Spirit doesn't absolutely prevent one from manifesting through a medium, and doing so in a previous earthly personality. One of our discarnate sources, a regular "visitor" while between lives, has reincarnated but still manifests occasionally; however, he says the added demands on his attention occasioned by his reincarnation take precedence.

ter things to occupy them than playing little experimental games with curious metaphysicists. Playing games is more the style of those entities who delight in leading us to erroneous conclusions.

This polishes off the final facet in this kaleidoscope chapter of the psychic and paranormal, which is intended to suggest how the nature and power of the superconscious mind—the "mind of the Spirit"—can account for a great variety of seemingly unrelated phenomena. Long though it is, this chapter nevertheless omits a great number of other mystical phenomena. Some of them I can't logically ascribe to the nature of the SC at my present stage of understanding; but if it can be convincingly shown that such disparate phenomena as those discussed here can be attributed to this common catalyst, it may be reasonable to tentatively assume that other paranormal happenings can be, too. Besides, this concept gives a neat explanation for orthodox science's frustration with metaphysics, as the next chapter points out.

Chapter 12

THE BEGINNING

. . . What's past is prologue. . . .
—Shakespeare
The Tempest

By now you must grant some credence to the possible existence of the superconscious mind. But other than any personal input you may have had from your own SC, you've probably found precious little verification elsewhere of the concept I've broached.

True, belief in a higher aspect—a Spirit or "soul"—is certainly commonplace, but it's usually conceived of as simply a nonphysical, perhaps divinely endowed, aspect that may survive physical death and serve as a carrier, or repository, of one's mortal personality and memories (from one or more lifetimes). But the idea that this aspect may possess an active intellect that is distinct from the recognized conscious mind is still not widely embraced, even though a number of individuals and organizations have declared its existence.

The Rosicrucians have taught the concept of a higher consciousness for at least three centuries. In the 1920's, Upton Sinclair's psychic wife, Craig, attributed ESP and clairvoyant talents to a third, or "deep" mind, as if some intelligent entity were directly informing her.[1] Cayce disseminated the concept and popularized the term *Superconscious* about a half century ago, while today many mystical disciplines use alternate terms such as the "higher self." Other mystics and organizations readily accept the independent intellect of the superconscious self as a personal "Spirit Guide," thinking it to be an "outside" source.[2] But not until science "discovers" the Superconscious will the concept gain respectability.

Fortunately, that may be on the horizon. Out of a study of hypnotism, that fascinating and little-understood route to nonconscious labyrinths of

---

[1] Prominent in literary circles during the first half of this century, Pulitzer Prize winner Upton Sinclair wrote some ninety books, including *Mental Radio* (New York: Macmillan Co., 1929). In a marked departure from his usual subjects, *Mental Radio* is a highly detailed and illustrated account of Craig's high success rate in ESP and clairvoyance experiments she engaged in over a number of years, and some theorizing about the psychic mechanisms involved. It is impossible to read this book without concluding that there is some validity to clairvoyance and ESP, or else that the Sinclairs are guilty of either fraud or collossal self-deception, neither of which I find plausible.

[2] "Spirit Guide" is one of those inexact terms with which metaphysics abounds. Certainly one's own Spirit, manifesting as the Superconscious, is a guide; but it's also true that some of us do receive guidance from other, "outside" Spirits.

mind, has come evidence to convince some serious researchers of the reality of multiple levels of perception and processing which function independently and simultaneously. Psychologist Ernest Hilgard, at Stanford University in the seventies, discovered and developed the concept of what is now called the "hidden observer," a level of perception and assimilation that seems to function separately from the "normal" conscious mind. Building on Hilgard's work, psychologist Jean-Roch Laurence of Canada's University of Waterloo says his research into the phenomena of duality and intuition is leading closer to an understanding of consciousness as being multileveled—that there are two control systems in the body, representing a split consciousness.[3]

Nowhere in the few accounts I've seen of scientific research into multilevel consciousness has the term "superconscious mind," been used, but the scientifically aseptic "hidden observer" isn't a bad substitute. For a beginning, although here we credit the superconscious mind with much more than mere observation; it may be a hidden persuader, a hidden dissuader, a subtle revelator, or a strong voice of conscience. But recognition by science of the occult (remembering that occult means hidden) observer is an encouraging first step.

If it's true that the SCs have been around for a few billion years, though, how come it's so tough to confirm their existence to the satisfaction of the

---

[3]See "Hypno Odyssey" by Paul Bagne in *Omni* Magazine, April 1985.

scientific community? Why do we seem to be just now seeing a few isolated researchers belatedly getting a glimmer of the higher intellect?

At least part of the answer is to be found in the innate nature of the quarry: it has a mind of its own! It *is* a mind of its own.

When the late Dr. J. B. Rhine began to research ESP phenomena at Duke University in the 1930s, he found that his best subjects—experimenters whose scores on card-"guessing" initially were significantly better than statistical average—seemed in time to lose their knack. And Craig Sinclair found her greatest percentage of "hits" occurred in the first three tries of any series. This inconstancy of ESP ability under test conditions is ammunition for the debunkers' denial of ESP: to be scientifically acceptable, a hypothesis under test must deliver consistent and repeatable results in laboratory experiments, but psychic phenomena consistently fail to be consistent. The result is frustration for ESP researchers, who uncover enough positive evidence in their firsthand endeavors to convince them of its reality but fail to obtain the consistency and repeatability necessary to convince secondhand observers. It's almost as though there is some influence at work that is motivated to thwart scientific proof.

Or that is susceptible to inhibition by the very presence and scrutiny of the doubter and the committed disbeliever. Some genuinely talented psychics excuse their failure to perform in the face of doubters' challenges by saying the "negative vibrations" accompanying their inquisitors inhibit their abilities; the challengers, of course, see this as a cop-out and smugly tout the fiasco as proof that such nonsensical concepts fail to stand up under controlled investigative conditions.

Although not necessarily attributing it to "negative vibrations," I observed an example of this kind of inhibition some years ago when late-night radio talk shows were daring enough to include the unconventional among their guests. A popular psychic making the rounds then was Dr. Gilbert Holloway, a genial ordained minister from Deming, New Mexico, whose ESP talent included the ability to discern the characteristics and circumstances of callers by simply hearing their voices. Counting his appearances on several stations, I probably have heard him "perform," using what he called the "Gift of the Spirit," for twelve or fifteen hours. On his "hot" nights, callers to the program gave him high marks for accuracy and, while some of his statements were overly general, others were quite specific. For instance, to a caller's breathless astonishment, he once alluded to her recent supermarket incident concerning S & H Green Stamps. He didn't make a practice of referring to Green Stamps; in fact, that was the sole time he did so in all the hours I've heard, so this can't be attributed to conicidence.

But I had to try Dr. Holloway for myself, so I called him on the Alan Douglas show on (then) WKYC, Cleveland, on the night of October 15, 1969. Upon hearing my voice and "reaching out to me in the Spirit," to use his standard phrase, he proceeded at some length to tell me about myself. I kept a point-by-point running tally of his stated perceptions. There were twenty points, of which I felt fourteen were quite correct ("I see you writing. I don't know what, but I see you writing late at night, night after night. . . ." That was correct; I was writing a book, mostly between 11:00 P.M. and 1:00 A.M.). Three were indeterminate or I was unable to judge them objectively e.g., "You are able to see both sides of a question" (I try, but am not sure I succeed), and three were clearly incorrect ("You are having some trouble with your left eye. . . ."). By discarding the indeterminate assertions, I judged him correct in fourteen of seventeen statements, for a score of better than eighty percent. Combining this with the accuracy attributed to him by other callers, I came away satisfied that Dr. Holloway did indeed have a valid claim to some ESP ability.

Alan Douglas was a model program host, maintaining an open and inquisitive attitude with his guests, no matter how "far out" their particular orientations might be. In this atmosphere, Dr. Holloway was able to display what I believe was a genuine ESP talent, even with some of the skeptical callers. And even sophisticated New York City audiences gave him high ratings during appearances with Long John Nebel on WNBC; on a November night in 1969, for instance, the average of the accuracy estimates given him by twenty callers was eighty-five percent, and none rated him below fifty percent. But Dr. Holloway was not so fortunate on the early morning of September 3, 1968, when he guested on the Barry Farber program on New York's WOR.

Farber claims to be susceptible to proof of the unorthodox, but seems in fact to be rather firmly

221

cemented to the rationality of orthodox science. Some of his regular fellow inquisitors on the program were less charitable in their commitment to disbelief, however, sometimes deriding guests to the point of vicious personal affront. On the day in question, Farber was accompanied by Felix Greenfield, who was then chairman of the Occult Research Committee of the International Brotherhood of Magicians and a highly committed skeptic.[4] He challenged Dr. Holloway to certain tests of clairvoyance, which Holloway willingly undertook and proceeded to fail soundly. His performance throughout the program was singularly disappointing to his supporters and no doubt greatly satisfying to Greenfield, who surely felt he had publicly unmasked another charlatan.[5]

Similar failures of psychic phenomena to manifest consistently under laboratory investigation continue to plague those researchers who attempt

_____

[4] It is interesting that virtually all professional illusionists are die-hard debunkers of the paranormal. Houdini spent a lifetime searching for a genuine spirit medium (there is some controversy as to whether he finally found one) and exposing frauds; more recently, Milbourne Christopher, Felix Greenfield, and James Randi ("The Amazing Randi") have been moved to strong public debunking.

Their basic premise is that they can duplicate any paranormal evidential phenomena through illusion. Since they consider the paranormal impossible, it follows that anyone else who displays seemingly impossible phenomena *must* also be resorting to the tricks of illusion and therefore is fraudulent, and they are incensed that the public is being "misled" by alleged psychics.

In refutation of their conclusion of inescapable fraud, I point out that just because phenomena *can* be manifested through illusion, it doesn't automatically follow that all such happenings *are*. For a simplistic example, the fact that one can simulate TV reception with suitably contrived motion-picture equipment doesn't alter the fact that actual TV transmission and reception is a reality.

[5] From my audio-tape files.

to codify and bring respectability to the field. In particular, when one researcher's carefully controlled experiments with a given subject are duplicated elsewhere by another scientist working with the same subject, it's practically a foregone conclusion that the results will not conform to those of the previous experiment. Because the test conditions are presumed to have been identical, the second researcher concludes that the first either misinterpreted or slanted his results; that the alleged psychic abilities of the subject are nonexistent.

What this assumption overlooks is the fact that the test conditions were *not* identical; that the second researcher is of a different mind-set (and perhaps different orientation at the superconscious level) and that the SC of the subject—the source of any psychic abilities the subject has—may for whatever reason choose not to play, just as Dr. Holloway's SC was driven by Felix Greenfield's covertly hostile attitude to refrain from performing.

If there's validity to our premise that all psychic happenings are workings of the superconscious mind, then it follows that laboratory research conducted in search of some neutral psychic "energy" that can be influenced directly and therefore consistently by a subject's conscious mind is misguided. Whether a psychic can perform at any given time is largely up to the free will, the temperament, even the whim of his/her SC and whatever restrictions may be placed on it by the rules of the Spirit domain. It is this unseen, unrecognized, and mostly unsuspected higher personality, which scientific researchers on either side of the controversy fail to take into account, that makes psychic manifestations unpredictable!

We have been told a number of times, by several of our sources: "Don't test the Spirits."[6] Most of them dislike "test" questions, often posed by a first-time recipient of a trance reading by asking questions to which he or she already knows the answer, just to see if the "reader" can come up with it.

I suppose it's understandable that the Spirits tire of having to prove themselves to every curious on-comer. If, as an experienced and capable driver, say, you had to pause at the entry to every town along a highway you were traveling and take a driving test before you were accepted on its streets, you'd soon tire of having to prove yourself. And it certainly would interfere with your progress toward your destination, wherever it might be. You would be inclined to bypass those towns, not caring in the least if they doubted your ability to drive. So it is with the Spirits: they generally don't care if others doubt them; *they* know they exist and have trans-physical powers, and they don't feel they have to prove anything. Why should they cooperate whole-heartedly in hour after hour of boring card-calling, or remote viewing experiments, or dice-influencing

---

[6] This does *not* mean you can't require satisfactory identification from an entity professing to be a departed friend or relative. When something of this nature manifests through a medium, automatic writing, or other mechanism, query it in depth and satisfy yourself that it is indeed who it claims to be. Remember that there are discarnate entities that manifest as imposters. Don't be taken in by them. Those who are genuine will not resent your checking to confirm their identities.

activities? No wonder psychics in the laboratory seem to diminish in their abilities as experiments drag on!

You might suppose that since each SC is a unique personality, that out of a few billion of them, there would be some who would be ham enough to *want* to put on carnival sideshows, thereby providing proof to all of their existence and their psychic ways. But there is more to the obfuscation of metaphysics than concerted distaste for theatrics by the SCs: they are subject to rules, too.

You may recall my statement that no psychic is *allowed* to be one hundred percent accurate (even if his SC could be, which is unlikely), because no mortal is permitted to be infallible. After all, an infallible mortal would come to be relied upon by the rest of humanity for total guidance, depriving us of the exercise of developing our own inner values and goals, one of the objectives of the mortal experience. An adjunct to this rule is that each person shall have the opportunity to develop *faith* in something that can't be conclusively incorporated into our physical reality structure. It may be faith in some unproven and unprovable conclusions of scientists or philosophers; or in some innate goodness of mankind; it may be faith in near and dear family; it may be faith in a deity; or it may be faith in one's self. Whatever it becomes for each individual, it is a requirement of this life that we must take some things on faith. We're here to grow, and we couldn't grow if everything were absolutely spelled out for us at the outset.

And so it is decreed that the existence of the

Spirit, and its key role in psychic phenomena, shall not in our lifetimes be explicitly revealed to the satisfaction of the orthodox scientific community, but shall be glimpsed, hinted at, and revealed to individual seekers as valid objects of their personal faith. In the meantime, researchers will continue striving to pin down the mechanisms of metaphysics, and will achieve some tantalizing breakthroughs, but I expect the controversy between materialists and visionaries to continue indefinitely because it has been decreed at some higher level. Now you know why, even after centuries of study, the world of the mystic remains elusive and scientifically unverifiable.

But that doesn't mean it doesn't exist. In its abstract sense, love is scientifically unverifiable, too, but we accept it, practice it, and make the world better with it. It may subjectively mean something different to each of us, but it is a positive force at its best. So is Spirituality. In fact, there may be a close relationship, if not identity, between love and Spirituality. So for those of us who can accept some personal reality on faith and experience the fruits it brings, scientific verification is unnecessary and we regret only that some zealous materialists try to ridicule away certain essential aspects of our personal reality. After all, as I said many chapters ago, if it *works* for you, it's real for you—regardless of what others may try to make you believe. And if the concept of the superconscious mind helps to explain phenomena beyond science for you, as it does for me, then to that extent at least, it works.

I believe that most persons who will wade through an entire book about psychic/metaphysical concepts entertain some desire to discern or develop psychic abilities of their own. Apart from suggesting that you seek contact with your own higher self in whatever way it may choose to manifest, I have not addressed the question of psychic development until now.

I first would ask *why* you might want to have psychic abilities? For some, it is a pure ego trip—an opportunity to perceive themselves as more capable, important, or talented than most. I don't view this as a commendable reason.

Psychic ability is widely perceived as a means to "know" the future, by many who seem to have a need to know what's going to confront them—good or bad—tomorrow and the week after. This can be a dangerous game, though, for several reasons: genuine precognitive talent is saddled with a very high error rate, so that for every accurate perception of the future there may be three inaccurate or misinterpreted ones; it's impossible for most to distinguish between visions of irrevocable future events (which some seem to be) and those probable ones that can be circumvented through redirection of present actions; and there is a tendency for one's prophecy-based expectations to become self-fulfilling, for better or worse. Some persons with precognitive ability consider it a mixed blessing at best, and a curse at worst.

Perhaps the greatest appeal psychic powers have for far too many people is that of personal advantage over others. Read the advertising in any publication touching upon the psychic and meta-physical and note that nearly all of it is phrased to appeal to self-centered desires. Buy a course in numerology and you can win state lotteries. Be guided by biorhythm charts and win at the races, or the sweepstakes, or whatever. Wear a certain charm or talisman and you will be instantly popular among your circle of acquaintances and co-work-ers. Study hypnotic techniques that give you the power to secretly command others to your bidding, or learn the secrets of psychically attracting a love partner. Use witchcraft spells to put a curse on your enemies. And on and on. Fortunately, few cus-tomers attain realization of those magical prom-ises—beyond the autosuggestive effects of belief, which evidently are sufficient to sustain their pur-veyors despite their generous money-back guaran-tees.

It's deplorable that the field of metaphysics should be perverted by blatantly commercial inter-ests using it for pandering to the prevalent human desires for wealth without effort and power without responsibility. This greed, feeding on gullibility, greatly compounds the problem of respectability for genuinely dedicated researchers and practitioners. To the casual skeptic, the whole genre seems to be comprised of charlatans turning a buck at the ex-pense of misguided believers intent on their own self-serving goals. I do not believe that the abilities of one's higher self are intended to be exploited for one's benefit if it is gained at the expense of others. There is a higher purpose inherent to the spiritual mind; one concerned with benefiting others as well as self. Because of this, many—probably the majority—of SCs simply will not cooperate in discreditable applications of psychic abilities.

This is not to say that a genuine psychic should never charge for services; after all, genuine services may be well worth their cost to the recipient. When you buy a service, you expect it to be as beneficial to you as the compensation is to the provider of the service. There's nothing wrong in a reasonable charge for a real service, and that applies as well to some psychics.[7]

Whether to charge is up to the individual conscience (or Superconscience) of the practicing psychic; for instance, Marianne believes she is not supposed to charge for the occasional personal readings she gives. Those "clients" expressing a desire to pay (and many feel her readings are worth a fee) are encouraged instead to donate as their conscience dictates to a children's charity. Conversely, other equally sincere and talented psychics manage to make their livings solely from fees, and we see nothing wrong in this so long as the fees aren't exorbitant. It's when the fascination of the public with the metaphysical is exploited purely for unjustified profit, through misrepresentation and appeal to unenlight-

---

[7]The psychic who relies for a living on compensation from clients may be plagued by the fact that psychic input is sporadic. When the psychic well dries up during a client's appointment, there is a strong temptation to "fake it," rather than to lose the fee for inability to "perform." History records many who, while having some genuine abilities, have felt it necessary to fake it to make a dollar or to save face and have been caught in their fraud, thereby destroying their hard-earned credibility. An ethical practitioner will admit to those times when input is withheld, and will refund any fees concerned.

ened self-interest, that great disservice is perpetrated in the name of metaphysics.

Another reason behind the interest some persons have in acquiring or developing psychic abilities can be defined as plain old curiosity. The desire to learn what lies behind those fascinating tales of improbable happenings is no different in principle from the curiosity that drives an explorer to search or a scientist to research. The delightful human desire to *know* the unknown fuels the passions of those who add to our cumulative store of knowledge. The baby destroys his rattle to learn what's making all the noise inside, and grows up to become an astronaut who gives his life to reach another planet. It's a story as old as civilization itself, and many of us turn our curiosity to the alternate realities of metaphysics. If we also happen to be so skeptical that we must experience for ourselves some of the phenomena alleged to manifest to others, then we entertain a desire to acquire personal psychic abilities—at least long enough to prove their reality. For there is nothing quite so convincing of the truth of the bizarre as to experience it firsthand.

Then there are the "chosen" ones; those who perceive the good they might be able to bring to others through some psychic gift. For these, altruism is the rule. Edgar Cayce is a notable example, having devoted so much unremunerated time to trance work intended to bring health and knowledge to others that he neglected his own health and departed too soon. And the late Olga Worrall, one of the most respected psychic healers of our time.

In common with ministers, nurses, counselors, and those dedicated to many other caring professions, some psychically talented persons respond to a self-less calling, and are strongly motivated to hone their psychic abilities to the maximum. Perhaps theirs is the most honorable reason for desiring to be psychic.

Before discussing how to "become" psychic, let's first address the question of whether it's possible. Can one who ostensibly has never precipitated a single psychic event somehow become telepathic, clairvoyant, or otherwise psychically sensitive?

Most psychics say yes. It's the general consensus among psychics that everyone possesses the necessary mechanisms, which are merely lying dormant in most of us. All we need to do, they say, is awaken those mechanisms, learn how to interpret them, and exercise them until we become confident and proficient. And this is understandable; finding abilities within themselves that seem in their experience to be ordinary, it's natural to suppose that everyone else is similarly endowed. Many individuals and organizations offer mail-order or resident courses, seminars, and books or tapes purporting to teach you how to become psychic. Most of these seem to be bonafide efforts to awaken you to your psychic abilities—which they may do, if you possess any.

But there may be restrictions imposed at higher levels. Astar firmly insists that no one can become psychic by choice; that the extent and nature of a particular individual's psychic abilities ("licenses," Astar says) is set by entities on higher levels and that you can study and practice till you're blue in the face and *never* learn how to be psychic, if you don't have the appropriate license from above.

This is an interesting, if unpopular, concept. Notice that Astar doesn't deny the possibility that you may discover and *refine* unsuspected, latent abilities for which you already have a license, but observation leads me to generally agree that not all of us are equal in inherent psychic talents, any more than all of us are equally endowed with a talent for music, or mathematics, or acting, etc. Members of our Metaphysical Research Group vary greatly in their characteristics and abilities, a few being highly psychic, the majority discerning certain psychic input to a limited degree, and a few denying even the slightest personal psychic experience. One delightful and dedicated member attended faithfully for three years without obtaining anything at all that she accepted as psychic. This failure certainly wasn't from lack of applying principles that worked for some others, nor from lack of belief; it seems she simply was not intended to have recognizable psychic talents.

At the other end of the spectrum, there's Marianne. If it's possible to learn to be psychic, one might expect that a person who is highly proficient in so many facets of the paranormal would have no difficulty attaining proficiency in another, but that's not the case with Marianne. She would very much like to extend her talents to include psychometry—obtaining knowledge through contact with a person's ring, locket, or other personal belonging—but in this area, she's an utter failure, despite much trying. Evidently her psychic "license" simply doesn't bear an endorsement for psychometry!

It's probably more than coincidence that many of those who become prominent in metaphysics, or in unique spiritual theologies (and if the source of all psychic events is the Spirit, then those events can be related to theologies) have undergone some explicit and singular event that seems to trigger their exceptional powers. Cayce had a visitation, as a boy, by a lady glowing with unearthly radiance. Psychic Peter Hurkos was seriously injured in a fall from a ladder and recovered to find himself newly psychic. Joseph Smith, founder of the Mormon movement, received a visitation from the discarnate Moroni. Richard Kieninger experienced numerous visitations during his puberty and adolescence, and went on to found the Stelle movement. Uri Geller had a boyhood visitation from a celestial being. Marianne should have died from a suicide attempt, but some higher influence intervened and she recovered to discover psychic abilities. And it's frequently reported in UFO lore that a participant in a close encounter later displays new psychic sensitivities.

While it's not clear in these relationships of singular incidents to psychic perceptions which is cause and which is effect, it does seem that pronounced psychic abilities are given to only some of us, often as a byproduct of some unique, improbable episode in our individual lives. The rest of us may have to settle for meager talents and study of those who are more fully "licensed."

While we may not be able to acquire talents we don't already possess, it's certainly true that most of us can sharpen those we do have. It appears that most of us have some receptivity to psychic input that we've failed all our lives to recognize or heed. This is where study, meditation, and guidance can be beneficial. A prime objective of Born/Astar in forming study groups was to bring to the membership an awareness of the Superconscious and a receptivity to its communications and manifestations, and by far the great majority of his students discovered in themselves some degree of psychic sensitivity; yet Born would be the first to deny vehemently that any of them had acquired and developed any psychic talents for which they hadn't been "licensed" long before.

So if you would like to have psychic talents, the first step is to explore your latent ones. The prime source for this is your Superconscious, which probably is most accessible during meditation. Honing your sensitivity to input from your SC is a basic step in searching out your latent talents, because that's where they reside. Get in touch with your higher self, and you're on the road to discovering and developing whatever level of psychic ability you may be permitted.

It also can be beneficial to affiliate yourself with some group of persons similarly seeking metaphysical truths. So long as they are not locked in a rigid, closed dogma, you can benefit from mutual

234

exploration.[8] But I would caution you to be sure of your own motivation. Is is simply to explore, learn, and broaden your own reality structure, or are you seeking some leader—some "authority by psychic revelation"—to hand you a ready-made paradigm, to make your decisions for you, to relieve you of responsibility for your own life? Unfortunately, some persons seek external objects and persons to blame or credit for their personal fates and fortunes, and some guru types are eager to accommodate them in organizations that become as misguided as the group of Jonestown infamy.

Given worthy motivation, you also will want to consider the possible personal risk in your search for personal psychic abilities. This is another area in which there is great disagreement; some teachers contend that there is only the risk of unleashing some of your own deeply repressed bogies, while at the other extreme is the assertion that *any* psychic involvement is trafficking with the devil. It's my belief that there is little risk to the mature searcher who is psychologically well-balanced and who invokes protective imagery such as the cocoon of white light or a prayer to God, but I do caution

---

[8] In this regard, belief—which is fundamental to successful application of psychic sensitivities—can be bolstered almost as strongly by observation as by first-person experience. To illustrate, in any group experimenting with such things as ESP, clairvoyance, etc., there will be one or two individuals who have exceptional success in a given experiment, while some others will totally fail (in a different test, it probably will be different individuals who excel). When you see a fellow classmate or two obtain astounding and unquestionable results under conditions where you *know* there was no cheating or duplicity, it is pretty convincing of the validity of a psychic event—even if your own performance met with utter failure.

you that *some individuals experience serious negative influences through psychic manifestation.* Some incidents are recounted in the next chapter.

As I have reiterated throughout this book, don't believe someone else's reality. It's your responsibility to formulate your own, because only you are responsible for your thoughts and actions, and they're directly influenced by your beliefs. Seek, search, weigh, accept, and reject. Study the countless beliefs interwoven with metaphysics and use those that work for you. And even if you never personally experience a psychic happening, you'll still benefit more than you can foresee by searching for communion with your Superconscious and the spiritual reality in which it operates.

Chapter 13

WHAT NOW?

He who should teach men to die would at the same time teach them to live.

—Michel de Montaigne
Essays. Book I. Chapt. 19

The effects of studying metaphysics can be insidious. Perhaps you take it up out of sheer intellectual curiosity about the "mysteries of mysticism," as I did, or maybe you are among those who fall prey to desire for the personal power over others promised by countless advertisements touting talismans, charms, books, or schools. Hopefully you are not among the latter, nor among those whose sense of inner inadequacy leads them to seek a guru or oracle to be responsible for their decisions and actions. But whatever your initial reason, a broad and open-minded study of the unseen worlds and your relationship to them is virtually guaranteed to change your life in some fundamental ways. There may be no wrenching outward change that raises your friends' eyebrows, but inwardly you will come to see your mortal-life goals in a different perspective that—subtly, at least—will influence your approach to life.

If you're familiar with the field of metaphysics, you've previously encountered variations on most of the concepts discussed in this book, with the possible exception of its keystone premise that the Superconscious is an intellectually distinct aspect of the mortal human to which attunement can be beneficial in this reality as well as others. As a sophisticate of metaphysics, you're in a position to weigh, compare, and select which concepts you find to be personally comfortable and which to discard.

On the other hand, if you're a newcomer to the subject, you've undoubtedly felt a number of your conventional concepts undergo considerable wrenching as you waded through the pages to this point; you may be on the verge of opening up to broader possibilities; and you may be looking for direction. Then this chapter is expressly for you.

If you happened to find the preceding chapters so explosively enlightening, so engrossingly convincing, so logically compelling that you think you've found the ultimate truth at last, watch out! Remember, I told you at the beginning not to believe this book! The fact that it postulates a number of concepts that happen to suit my present structure of practical reality doesn't mean you're to adopt them uncritically as your own truths. This whole exercise is intended to challenge you; to open you to consideration of the metaphysical; to spur you into the growth that comes only from your own research into the nature of realities beyond and the conclusions you draw therefrom. In the process, I've revealed and emphasized that aspect of you that I believe to be your greatest authority for validation of your belief structure: your own Superconscious. Don't take another's word as law; listen to your higher self!

If I've managed to drive this single point home, I may have coaxed you into a position falling between two extremes: unbridled gullibility, on the one hand, versus unyielding anchorage to conventional materialism on the other. Somewhere midway between these is the delicate balance of open-minded skepticism. Skepticism of the sort possessed by John G. Fuller, author of several carefully researched books on specific paranormal episodes. He defines himself as a "benevolent skeptic," as opposed to a "destructive skeptic" who persuades people to "dismiss all evidence out of hand."[1] So don't believe this book; view it and all others with benevolent skepticism and become your own authority.

So there you sit, with your benevolent skepticism and your curiosity and an inoculation of metaphysical concepts. Astral realms . . . reincarnation . . . Spirit entities. . . . Maybe death won't be so full of surprises when it strikes, but with any luck, that's somewhere in the indefinite future. What about *now?* Does any of this have immediate significance, application, and benefit in the real, everyday world? How does one incorporate these

---

[1] Reported by Brian McKernan in *Omni* Magazine, October 1984.

concepts into daily routine? What are the choices—and the consequences that accompany them?

One obvious choice is to *do nothing*. That's the safe, comfortable way to preserve the sense of security that comes with belief only in the tangible, mechanistic, and finitely bounded world recognized and catalogued by orthodox science. Metaphysical concepts and psychic influences may have no place in your life beyond mere intellectual curiosity about the crazy beliefs of some other people. You probably can live the rest of this lifetime in a self-limiting personal reality, completely oblivious to higher existences and alternate realities—but if it happens to be true that you are here to grow spiritually, then you'll be missing the boat this time around, won't you? I'm confident that you are *not* a do-nothing, or you wouldn't have reached this point in the book.

Then there's the opposite extreme: *asceticism*. You can take the purported existence of spiritual goals as a mandate to withdraw totally from crass materialism and devote your every remaining mortal moment to intense meditation, prayer, fasting, self-denial, seclusion, and abject servitude to the concept of self-negation. You may learn to sit high on a frigid Himalayan plateau, clad only in a robe, and perspiringly melt a circle of ice into water with nothing but your body heat, or to levitate yourself in apparent defiance of gravity, or survive with suspended animation in a grave, all showing great mastery of mind over matter—or Spirit over flesh, if that's your perception. This may make you feel purified and spiritually elevated, but it certainly removes you from the real purpose of mortal existence: to learn, over as many lifetimes as it may take, to interact with your fellow mortals in genuine brotherhood. For this, in my view, is the real *raison d'être* for all religions. The carrot to inspire it may be salvation, nirvana, ascent to Heaven, or what-have-you, but the *real* function of the social structure, of the models of morality set forth by any of the established religions is to lubricate relationships *in this mortal reality* against the frictions that naturally arise in a society of egocentric, free-willed humans; to provide guidelines for respecting the person imbued with that sanctified corpuscle that resides, however obscurely, within every human being. This amounts to a call for us to cultivate *love* in its broadest sense for every person, and to apply it in every social interaction. Psychic investigator and writer Harold Sherman lists love as a pivotal concept—a commandment—of twelve of the world's major religions,[2] which form the bases of belief for most of the world's population. The ascetic who retires from society to pursue his own private exercises in "purification" surely is socially unproductive and is neglecting his mortal opportunities. I trust you're not drawn to asceticism.

Having discarded the extremes from consideration for "what now," here is a more reasonable and practical suggestion: allow some early time for *reflection*. If most of the concepts of metaphysics are new to you, take as long as you need to digest them; to turn them over and over in your mind if necessary and examine their relationship—and their threat—to those belief structures that you may never before

---

[2] *How to Know What to Believe.* Fawcett Books, New York, 1976.

have questioned. There's no hurry about this; no urgency to conclusively accept any dogma. If it's time for you to enlarge your conceptual and spiritual horizons, you shortly will find doors opening and inviting you to learn in depth. If it isn't, then simply bide your time, put these concepts in storage for later reexamination, and let the future take care of itself. Don't make the mistake of some newcomers to metaphysics, who become carried away in the excitement and fascination of nonphysical realms of existence, uncritically accept the first new concepts they encounter as great new truths to live by, and prematurely abandon the inner reality structures that have served them adequately in the past. Remember that our definition of valid subjective reality is that which *works* for you. Don't forsake what has worked, until—through tentative trial and evaluation—you assemble a structure that works better. If you exercise this precaution, there is little danger of your becoming a slavish and unthinking convert to some self-styled guru or cult leader, or in abandoning a workable philosophy for one that ultimately proves disastrous.

If you approach the subject with Sherman's "benevolent skepticism," you'll want to explore the multitude of metaphysical concepts in more variety and more detail than this book provides. There are a few precautions that should be considered before you jump in with both feet; there is some merit in the biblical injunctions against involvement in the subject. If we postulate the existence of discarnate entities, and attribute to them the power of free will, it is a virtual certainty that some of those entities

242

harbor intentions that are less than commendable. In other words, there *are* shady characters in the astral realm—some of whom apparently are poised to manifest in some fashion when given an opening. It behooves you to keep yourself closed to them.

This statement is disputed by many in metaphysics, as well as most in conventional psychiatry, who contend that the only negative influences are in the minds of mortal humans. These will ridicule my warnings against opening to negative external entities and will assert that there's no risk of encountering anything more insidious than your own deeply repressed subconscious imagery and phobias when you dabble in the occult. Our sources, though, insist that there *are* astral entities with mischievous and even nefarious intentions; certainly, they say, there are mis-motivated Spirits, and they hint at other, subhuman, entities that can be loosely described as ''elementals'' or ''demons.''

From this, we have to be circumspect by advising precautions against falling under the influence and misguidance of negative entities that may exist. The precautions can do no harm, even if it should happen that they are unnecessary. Invoking the ''cocoon of white light'' suggested in Chapter 14 can be effective and certainly is harmless.

There is a variety of mechanisms through which contact with discarnate entities may be made. They can be useful to seasoned metaphysicists for obtaining alleged truths about the ''other side''—the astral realm, but they are best approached with caution by the neophyte. Paramount among these is the Ouija board, sold everywhere as a mere game of amusement, without a warning hint of potential hazard. To describe the Ouija board, if you're not familiar with it, it consists of a board with the letters of the alphabet, numbers from one through zero, and the words *yes*, *no*, and *good-bye* (note that its name is made up of "yes" in French plus "yes" in German). In use, a gliding platform called the planchette is moved about so its pointer or window identifies each letter or number (or word) in turn to spell out messages. Conventionally, two players place their hands lightly on the planchette and wait for an impulse to move it—and, when anything intelligible is spelled out, usually each accuses the other of volitionally pushing it. We have found that a single operator, if a sensitive, can operate the board equally as well. The operator usually describes the process either as feeling mysterious urges to move the planchette about and consciously responding, or perhaps as though the arm muscles actually are controlled directly by an unseen force. For many, the Ouija board never succeeds as more than a parlor game, but others do, indeed, receive a variety of fascinating, puzzling, nonsensical, or cryptic messages from some source.

Psychologists—those few who will concede that the Ouija board may in fact produce messages from other than the consciousness of an operator—tend to attribute such messages to that operator's subconscious mind. This may be true for some, and it may also be that plumbing the murky depths of one's subconscious can be as alarming as any manifestation by a discarnate entity of ill intent. On the other hand, the literature is filled with references to individuals who found themselves misled and in rare cases even temporarily overwhelmed by *something* malevolent manifesting through their Ouija boards; often something revealing knowledge that couldn't possibly have been in their subconscious (in their current lifetime experience). It is my understanding that it was a Ouija board that first captivated the child whose real-life episode inspired Peter Blatty's *The Exorcist* a few years ago (although the principal in the novel was a girl, it was a twelve-year-old boy who had the actual experience underlying the story, in 1949–50). According to the Reverend John Nicola, technical consultant for the filming of *The Exorcist*, the boy's mother perceived the planchette moving about on the Ouija board when *nobody* was touching it—which must have been highly unnerving by itself.[3] Whether the boy actually was "possessed" by one or more discarnate entities or was exceedingly disturbed by intense manifestations from his subconscious is more or less beside the point of this particular topic; whichever, the door to severe trouble seemed to be opened by his playing with a Ouija board.

We have firsthand knowledge of another individual who suffered prolonged and severe anxiety resulting from messages she received through her Ouija board. In this case, the entity sending the messages identified itself as God! This alone would immediately raise a red flag in the mind of any seasoned metaphysicist; God is not noted for manifesting through Ouija boards. But if you devoutly

[3]Related by Father Nicola, author of *Diabolical Possession and Exorcism*, at a Consciousness Frontiers seminar on March 28, 1981, at Northern Virginia Community College, Sterling, VA.

believe in God and you receive messages purporting to be from God, do you dare to question their authenticity? If by even the remotest chance they actually were from God, you'd be risking His disfavor to doubt their authenticity. This is asking a lot from a newcomer to metaphysics.

Not only was she shaken by their alleged source; the messages were alarming in content, rather than uplifting. At first they were prophetically accurate, seeming thereby to establish the authenticity of their supernatural source; then when distressingly dire predictions were later made, the unfortunate woman was extremely troubled by her expectations of impending, inescapable disaster. She forsook the Ouija board, but by then she had become susceptible to direct manifestations in her mind. She was warned away from friends who could have been supportive and reassuring, and she suffered severe anguish in virtual isolation. In time, as the more deadly predictions turned out to be unfounded, her fear of their infallibility and her emotional disturbance slowly subsided—but her life has been permanently marked by this highly negative experience that began with innocent but injudicious use of the Ouija board.

Because an essential step in the Ouija experiment is your mental invitation to external entities to manifest through you and through your hands on the planchette, you are actually offering an opening into your own psyche for any entity that may be lurking on the coincident astral plane for just such an opportunity. If you recall the analogy in Chapter 3 of the pilot in the cockpit of his plane, you will appreciate that you would not choose to turn over your flight to a "guest" pilot of unknown qualifications and destination; yet this is directly comparable to incautiously inviting other entities to manifest through you to operate the Ouija board. If you're a newcomer to metaphysics, it will be prudent for you to postpone involvement with the Ouija board until you are seasoned enough to effectively employ protective precautions with it.

Another mechanism by which we believe external entities manifest through living human "channels" is automatic writing. In this case, the "receiver," a sensitive, simply sits with paper and pencil; the entity seems to literally take control of the receiver's arm muscles to write its messages. Usually the handwriting is totally different from that of the sensitive, and the syntax and grammar may be from another era. In some cases, the sensitive may be in deep trance and have no recollection of what was written until it is read; in others, the sensitive may feel that actual control of the arms is taken directly by the manifesting entity; and a third variation is for the sensitive to volitionally move the arm and hand according to subtle mental urges. Metaphysical literature is rife with entire books purported to have been written by "higher" entities through the mechanism of automatic writing.

Automatic writing in all its variations, like the Ouija board, entails the opening of one's psyche to outside entities and, while experiments in automatic writing seem to give a lower rate of success among beginning metaphysicists than occurs with the Ouija board, the risks of undesirable manifestations are probably as great for the uninitiated and

247

should best be postponed until one is better equipped to exclude them.

Most of the other "common" methods by which contact is made with discarnate entities don't involve an "invitation to enter" and probably hold less risk for most newcomers to metaphysics. Among these is consultation with Spirit mediums, through whom alleged other entities speak while the medium is in some level of trance. The common perception is that such manifesting entities are from the realm of the deceased, but in fact it apparently is possible for the Superconscious of a living person to manifest through a medium, too, even despite great geographical separation of the two individuals. As an observer, you may watch such phenomena manifesting in others without being at any great personal risk yourself.[4] Just remember to maintain your benevolent skepticism.

Your first experience of witnessing a genuine trance medium at work can be a bit eerie and sometimes convincingly impressive; with further observation, however, you'll soon learn that not everything received in this manner is what it purports to be, and you become more discriminating in your judgments. In my case, that revelation came by radio. In the sixties, when the late Long John Nebel hosted all-night talk shows on New York's WNBC

---

[4] It is highly unlikely that a beginning metaphysicist will suddenly perform as a trance medium, although having one's *own* SC speak while in trance is entirely possible—and is not to be feared; this is not mediumship, but a manifestation of one's higher self. And if you can't trust your *own* higher self, you're hopelessly adrift and had better steer clear of the whole gamut of psychic things until you develop some faith in yourself!

radio (and WOR before that), he had as guests many who were involved in the "fringe" areas of reality— UFO contactees, psychics, cultists, and writers and researchers of all persuasions. One night he aired *two* "seances" that he had recorded earlier on separate occasions. Each featured a different, regionally prominent medium, both of whom were charged with going into trance and contacting the Spirit of Rudolph Valentino! Each ultimately seemed to succeed in reaching some entity claiming to be Valentino, whereupon Long John plied it with a list of prepared questions. He used the same list in both sessions, and then subsequently broadcast both seances, back to back, in the same program.

Having at that time never experienced a seance, I listened in rapt fascination. My first conclusion was that indeed *something* was going on; the mediums' sincerity and the changes in voice, breathing, and accent as the intermediary "Spirit Guides" manifested and then the alleged personality of Valentino came through sounded pretty convincing. But was this really what it seemed?

Had I heard only one of the two seances, I might have tentatively concluded that I had truly witnessed messages from Valentino. The difficulty arose from hearing both in sequence, though, because the alleged Valentino gave greatly different answers to the same questions on the two occasions! It was clear that at last one of them was an impostor, playing games with the medium and us.[5] Thus did I learn, relatively painlessly, that not

---

[5] Of course *both* could be impostors.

everything "spiritual" is exalted and uplifting. Conversely, the experience didn't turn me away with a conviction that *all* seances are either fraud or manifestations of the devil, either. It only made me cautious and more curious.

Orthodox science, of course, ridicules the whole concept of seances and other "supernatural" happenings. Lest you fall into the same trap of unqualified contempt for science that many metaphysicists do, I want here to suggest that you not accept metaphysics at the expense of your established belief in physics; i.e., don't discredit scientific knowledge out of hand. This may seem contradictory at first thought, but it is my conviction that as we research further into the real truths underlying both scientific and metaphysical endeavors, they will—ultimately—converge onto common ground.

This may surprise you. For example, earlier in this book I made comments that might seem to denigrate the theory of evolution of the species. To the contrary, however, I accept as irrefutable the hard evidence for what appear to be progressive steps in the evolution of animal forms. That there are fossils of extinct species evidently bridging some of the steps from one species to another is an undeniable fact. I do not deny the hard evidence, but I do take issue with the conclusion that this all happened by fortuitous chance and subsequent natural selection. Rather, I find the concept of *directed* evolution, wherein the incremental steps from one "model" to another—many of which simply could not have happened gradually because a viable continuum would be impossible—were in some fashion instigated by a guiding intellect, to be a more rational one. Scientists, because they can't yet detect, measure, or replicate the presence or the influence of such a guiding intellect and cannot, under the rules of science, declare its existence, are left with the less satisfactory explanation for what the fossil record undeniably shows. The *evidence* is not in question, but science's *conclusions* sometimes may be. This is not to denigrate scientists, but to point out that their knowledge still is incomplete.

But so is that of the more zealous creationists. The fossil record doesn't necessarily deny the possibility of divine creation but it does prove (to me) that it didn't occur in six days as we measure time. It also proves that man has been around in some physical form for a lot more than the six thousand years or so that some of the hard-line Bible literalists believe. Unless, of course, God and His minions intentionally created false remains of prehistoric life and abrupt discontinuities in carbon's rate of radioactive decay just to test our acceptance of one man-written document in preference to the overwhelmingly contrary (planted?) physical evidence. Frankly, I find such imputed deviousness by God to be far more improbable, illogical, and unworthy of Him, than is the possibility that the Bible may be symbolic rather than literal insofar as creation is concerned. In my personal reality structure, belief in the Godhead does not necessitate belief in a six-day creation.

So I think the metaphysicist should respect the factual knowledge of science and, rather than debunk it out of hand, examine it to see how it may support and even enhance our metaphysical concepts. The truly open-minded scientist will be the first to concede that science doesn't know everything. Nothing is more subject to change and evolution than scientific belief. For instance, Newton developed and quantified the laws of motion as he perceived them, and those laws were valid ("true") insofar as physicists could detect in Newton's time. They worked, and they still work in the gross practical world today. Then along came Einstein with a theory that refined Newton's laws, adding a second-order term to take account of a body's velocity relative to the velocity of light. This special theory of relativity corrects for incremental inadequacies in Newton's equations that come to light when very high physical velocities are involved.[6] And that's more or less the technique of science: to derive explanations for observed events that will work to replicate them, and then pronounce these explanations as fact—until new evidence forces reexamination and revision of those explanations, whereupon old "truths" are displaced. This is the evolution of scientific "fact"; obviously it's more charitable to recognize that scientists' beliefs at any time are based on incomplete knowledge (as are

---

[6] It also suggests that nothing in our physical reality can be accelerated beyond the velocity of light and, conversely, that any body already traveling faster than light relative to our reality would be completely undetectable by us and therefore would not exist in this reality, even though it's perfectly solid in its own reality. I consider it unfortunate that most scientists have accepted the velocity of light as an absolute limit; I anticipate that one day someone will derive a third-order or higher term to add to Newton's equations that will suggest ways to break the light-velocity barrier, but it's unlikely to happen so long as science perceives that barrier to be impervious.

the metaphysicists'!) than to discount them altogether. *That scientific evidence which undeniably exists cannot be scorned;* it must be accepted by the metaphysicist, even though his interpretation of its significance may differ from the scientists'.

Thus far in this chapter on "what now," we've examined mostly "not-to-dos." Don't rush to embrace the first metaphysical dogma you find; don't open yourself up to unknown entities via the Ouija board, automatic writing, or direct mediumship until you are prepared to invoke proper safeguards; don't reject valid scientific evidence because the Establishment theories allow no room for the supernatural. . . . Now it's time to turn from negatives to some positive directions.

Certainly one of the safest approaches to familiarity with the world of metaphysics is plain old *reading.* You run little risk of encountering threatening entities or alarming circumstances in the pages of a book, although it is possible to suffer from the guru-worship syndrome if you are so captivated by one author's assertions that you lose your benevolent skepticism and fail to weigh those assertions against those by other individuals having comparable credentials. Given the variety of paranormal manifestations ascribed to metaphysics (and all the other "fringe" areas of experience and belief that may also be metaphysical manifestations) and given the centuries during which mankind has been observing these things, there is a resulting abundance of written material to occupy the newcomer to the field. An overwhelming abundance, in fact; so much that a beginner finds selection quite difficult. So is making a recommendation for beginners and, since I don't wish to bore you with page after page of book titles, I will simply recommend—in addition to this book—your local library and book store.

As this is written, I know of two periodicals devoted to the field that may be found on selected newsstands or in some book stores. They are quite different in their approaches to metaphysics.

Fate Magazine oddly mixes archaeological reports having no metaphysical significance with others covering the gamut of the psychic/occult/supernatural, written largely by professional and free-lance authors, independent investigators, and readers. Most articles are reportorial and anecdotal, rather than tutorial. Published monthly, *Fate* is an interesting doorway for someone seeking to explore the range of metaphysical phenomena. But while the magazine claims newsstand availability, you may have to subscribe in order to obtain it regularly. You'll certainly have to exercise your benevolent skepticism as you read it, but the ads in its pages are an education by themselves! A fascinating sideshow of fantastic inducements and blatant promises leaves the first-time reader utterly amazed by this colorful fringe area of commercial enterprise of which most of the public is blissfully ignorant. If ever a single publication presented a good sampling of the breadth of activities encountered in the occult/metaphysical and the chaos of often contradictory philosophies attempting to ex-

---

[7]Clark Publishing Co., 500 Hyacinth Place, Highland Park, IL 60035.

plain them, that publication must be any issue of *Fate*. Incidentally, a number of specialty book stores advertise in the magazine, offering far greater depth and variety in metaphysical books than you'll find in conventional book stores.

Psychic Guide[8] is a quarterly publication claiming readership in excess of a half million. It differs markedly from *Fate* in its editorial thrust, with most of its articles authored by a small staff of contributing editors, and by a coterie of psychic practitioners who also are advertisers of their services in its pages. Most pieces presume to be tutorial, explaining the metaphysical structures of the various practitioners' specialties or answering readers' questions, and they're often couched confidently in "this-is-the-real-and-only-truth" terms. I am sometimes put off by their inappropriate cocksureness regarding phenomena for which I know there are various possible explanations, and I find some articles appear to be self-serving promotions for their authors' commercial psychic enterprises. I believe I prefer *Fate*'s separation of editorial and commercial content.

My caveats aside, *Psychic Guide* is another door for exploring the world of metaphysics. As with *Fate*, this book, and all other publications, you must weigh what you read in it and draw your own conclusions. You might also find something of interest in the magazine's large "Bookshop" section, listing books on a great variety of subjects. *Psychic Guide* may be found at many specialty book stores.

After you have read widely enough to acquaint

[8]P.O. Box 701, Providence RI 02901.

yourself with the field of metaphysics, you probably will wish to find others with whom to explore concepts and discuss theories. In larger cities, there always are several groups of varying dedication, size, and flexibility of dogma, but they may be virtually invisible. If there is a specialty book store or occult shop, it almost certainly will have a bulletin board or other directory of meetings and activities by the various groups, from which you can contact the organizations. Most are glad to receive persons with similar interests and will extend you membership for some nominal fee. Joining those that seem most compatible with your views is a rewarding way to meet others with similar interests. I would caution you once more, though, to maintain your benevolent skepticism and reinforce your independence of thought with respect to any organization; it is the leaders of such groups that sometimes suffer from a God complex and seek to turn their organizations into cults.

It may be that there are no established metaphysical study groups in your home town—in which case you may want to make an effort to start one. All it takes is locating another person or two with curiosity and interests similar to yours. I believe any town with more than a dozen people will harbor a few closet metaphysicists; all you have to do is flush them out. Maybe nothing more than a discreet personal ad in the local newspaper, promising confidentiality, will do it. Or boldly interspersing exploratory test comments in your everyday conversation with likely prospects will reveal their secret interest in such things.[9] The whole business of researching metaphysics is a lot more fun when you interact directly with others having like interests.

For most of us, pursuit of metaphysics sooner or later outgrows the mere curiosity stage. Finding in the literature a wealth of accounts by respected and credentialed witnesses, and/or personally observing a number of manifestations strongly supporting the existence of sentient entities in nonphysical states, you come to recognize that the spiritual or transcendental aspects of reality revealed thereby must spill over into your basic philosophy of life and the way you conduct your everyday activities. For example, it seems obvious that one who believes in physical death as the absolute end of a purely mortal entity surely is going to live that life differently than is one who believes that the personality survives in some ongoing form and that he may be held accountable at some time by some higher authority. Perhaps the former individual values material possessions most highly and feels secure that his unethical actions which remain concealed from other mortals can never work to his detriment; the latter, recognizing within the structure of his belief that material possession is only transitory—"you can't take it with

---

[9]Be advised that your stereotype of "likely prospects" probably is useless. Individuals indulging interest in the metaphysical are as varied as people in general. Our groups have attracted professionals such as doctors, lawyers, engineers, teachers, nurses, policemen, actors, etc.; teenagers and retirees; the wealthy and impecunious; male and female; married and single—practically the whole gamut of human characteristics. It's often surprising to find that someone you've always considered to be totally pragmatic and conventional harbors a secret interest in the existence of intangible realities.

you"—may set different mortal lifetime goals. Not the least, for some, is development of a personal code of conduct based on inner values rather than on mere conformance for the sake of appearance. The fact that this self-censoring concept may arise from a belief that you ultimately will be called by higher authority to account for even your most private actions—and even your consciously nurtured thoughts![10]—doesn't negate its significance; the personal integrity it lends to all situations you encounter is nevertheless an attribute.

For some of us, this starts early. My childhood belief, based on Sunday-School teachings, was that God was minutely aware of our every thought and deed; at a later age, when it grew to seem likely that God had neither the time nor inclination to concern Himself (on a moment-by-moment basis, at least) with the most insignificant details of our most mundane activities, there still was the concept of a "book of life" in which all those details could be discerned later, upon one's application for admission to Heaven—and surely *someone* was recording them in it. Then there was also my concept of my Spirit counterpart; perhaps *it* was keeping the diary. In any event, I have spent my life, practically as far back as I can remember, with the sensation that someone is looking over my shoulder; that there's nothing I

[10] The idea that one should police even one's thoughts strikes some people as a novel and disturbing concept. Yet this surely was a major tenet of Christ's teaching: that one should develop attitudes of *thought* that lead to a strong inner-value structure of self-discipline. "As you think, so shall you become." Remember that nothing, including character, is created without first having been conceived in thought.

can really hide. It's a great way to develop a sense of self-discipline and self-esteem that discourages violations of inner values. It doesn't matter that no one else may ever know when I transgress; *I* know, and that's uncomfortable enough to make me abide by my own values with high consistency. The much more recently acquired understanding of the presence and role of my Superconscious only tends to confirm the presence I have intuitively felt all my life, and the moral and ethical guidance I have gained by respecting it. That understanding also tends to reestablish a variation of the old Sunday-School concept of God's personal awareness of each human; the "corpuscle of God" inherent in each Superconscious can be construed as one's personal "piece" of God. This higher intellect is aware of, concerned with, and a guiding influence to, each mortal. The Godhead may not directly observe your every action, but its representative does, and your record is there in your superconscious memory for the sharing with such other entities as your SC deems necessary.[11] The moral of all this is that you may hide your actions from other mortals, but you can't hide them, or even your thoughts, from your*self.* And it is yourself—at all levels—that you have to live with, so you find yourself striving to live up to *your* standards,

---

[11]A concept found in Eastern religions is that of the *Akashic Records,* a sort of nonmaterial "library" in which records of every activity of every human are somehow stored and available to those who know how to access the "files." This is in addition to the living memories stored within each superconscious intellect, and our sources confirm that there is in fact something resembling the Akashic Records. So there may be more than one source for revealing of all your life's thoughts and deeds.

which are likely in time to become more demanding than those of others.

And what of all this new sense of self-responsibility? Will it be instrumental in changing your goals in life? Will it impinge in some fashion on your very day-to-day lifestyle? As usual, the answers are up to you.

Probably the most common enlargement of personal perspective results from the strong evidence for the factual existence of realms peopled by discarnate entities, no matter how invisible, undetectable, and inadmissible they may be to hard science. If there are such places and such entities, then the concepts of one's individual spirit aspect and continuation of life in some form following mortal death become more than just a psychological wish-fulfillment fantasy. If you were a believer before, your belief becomes elevated a few steps closer to certainty; if you were doubtful, your doubts grow smaller. Either way, it is impossible for you to undergo this change in perspective without affecting the way you rank your goals in life.

Many of us who feel we have unearthed great new truths from our study of metaphysics develop a desire to share them with the whole world. After all, here is enlightenment which, once shared by everybody, could move this imperfect world well along the road to Paradise—and we tend to presume that, of course, everyone is just waiting in his innocent ignorance to be enlightened through sharing our knowledge. So we form study groups, and expect them to grow geometrically as revelation permeates their ranks. Or we write books, not for the royalties, but for the satisfaction of spreading knowledge. And we become disenchanted when the study groups dwindle to zero or books aren't grabbed off the counters by the millions. But the *real* value of our enlightenment lies in our applying it in our everyday activities—in respecting the dignity and innate sanctity of all others; in helping individuals in small ways when the opportunity presents itself, whether simply by encouragement, lending a sympathetic ear, suggesting a different way of looking at a difficult situation, or whatever your particular talents may provide. Small kindnesses on a one-to-one basis probably are all that most of us are destined to perform this time around—but the cumulative effect of even these over a lifetime can be significant. And this is what it's all about. To discipline one's free will so that one's inner values are consistent with the dignity and sanctity of all humankind—including yourself—is the fundamental purpose of the physical experience, and your growing understanding of metaphysics and alternate realities will underline that purpose. Live from this point on in full awareness of transcendent realities, and the only surprises death may bring are bound to be pleasant ones.

Chapter 14

A MEDITATION EXERCISE

As promised earlier in this book, here is an introduction to meditation.

I say "introduction" because these remarks are aimed at those who are newcomers, so to speak—who are just beginning to explore the techniques and benefits of meditation. If it happens that you're an old hand at meditation—that you already have settled on a concept and method that works for you—stay with it. If this is the case, you won't need this.

Incidentally, it's certainly not necessary to believe in the superconscious mind, enlightenment, or any other metaphysical concept addressed in this book to partake of the benefits of meditation. Millions of persons engage in daily meditation routines of one sort or another for the real and immediate physical and emotional recentering it can provide, and many of them would scoff at most metaphysical beliefs.

Here we'll examine what meditation is, some of the things you may be able to do with it, and a few simple techniques to get you started on your own exploration of meditation and the inner realities it may reveal to you. Much of this material is adapted from a meditation tape I produced for use with the local Metaphysical Research Group.

So, what *is* meditation? Many things to many people. According to an old dictionary, it's the act of continuous thinking, or absorbed contemplation, or a devotional exercise consisting of dwelling in thought upon a religious or ethical precept. Well, it may be any of those, but I use the word here in a very broad sense to mean a method or exercise to achieve:

a. beneficial physical relaxation, at the very least;
b. a clearing of incidental mind clutter so as to focus on your choice of the meditation objectives I'll describe in a few moments.

Meditation is really an exercise in *centering*; that is, in bringing your physical, mental, emotional, and spiritual aspects into a sort of holistic harmony, or unity, with which you can explore the new possibilities that this integration of the whole you opens up.

Now if that sounds a little like high-flown double talk, I hasten to point out that there are some very real, scientifically measurable effects of meditation. While we don't yet have the instruments to measure your spiritual status, we can measure definite physiological changes resulting from meditation. For example, the first step in any method of meditation is to engage in total physical relaxation. The purpose is to clear your mind as much as possible of the distractions that physical sensations and minor discomforts create, but measurable benefits include reduced blood pressure and diminished muscular tensions. The interesting part is that, while these changes are brought on during meditation, they actually last for as much as several hours afterward, so that if you meditate for just a few minutes twice a day, your physical self benefits practically all day long. This is an observable and measurable result that alone makes meditation worthwhile.

Another effect of meditation is revealed by the electroencephalograph—the EEG, a measure of electrical activity in the brain. Neurologists classify the pulsating brain-wave potentials they record with the EEG in four broad categories: beta, alpha, theta, and delta. These occur in various relative proportions, depending on one's mental state at any moment.

Beta waves, those repeating from about fourteen to thirty times a second, are dominant when you're fully alert and applying your mind to whatever is the task at hand.

Alpha waves, occurring from about eight to thirteen times a second, become dominant during certain stages of sleep, but they also accompany daydreaming, psychic trance states, and some stages of hypnosis—and meditation.

Theta waves, those from four to seven cycles per second, are related to certain levels of sleep and of hypnotic trance, while delta waves, from one half to three and one half cycles, represent the very deepest sleep, bordering on comatose.

I want to emphasize that these brain-wave designations—alpha, beta, etc.—are not some esoteric metaphysical terminology, but represent real, measurable electrical signals, accepted and classified by medical science. And we have learned that it is in the conscious *alpha* state that we are most open to intuition, inspiration, guidance from our higher self, or exercise of psychic ability, so an elementary goal of meditation is to withdraw the mind from beta-level activity and open it to those capabilities existing at the alpha level. You can learn to shift to alpha at will, and meditation is an exercise in doing just that. An EEG taken during meditation will confirm that this physiological change does indeed occur.

Or, to express it in terms of the popular concept of right-brain/left-brain specialization, meditation is an exercise to put the analytical left brain on idle, clearing the way for the intuitive right brain to manifest. While the validity of the alleged right-brain/left-brain differences has come under fire, it's still a convenient model for visualizing distinctive modes of mental activity.

Obviously, bodily relaxation procedures for entering meditation can bring some physical benefits, but how does shifting the brain to the alpha state fit in? Well, the possible mental, or emotional, or experiential results attainable from the alpha state *can* be highly beneficial—even more so than the physical. And there are several directions you can go.

The traditional concept of meditation presents it as an exercise in *passivity*; a clearing of the mind and waiting for something—inspiration, solutions, enlightenment, a personal message from God—to just drop into it. Indeed, many famous creative persons have relied on meditative or dream states for inspiration. You may find this is all you want from meditation.

My preference is for *directed* meditation; that is, going into the exercise with a specific objective. Perhaps you seek an answer within yourself to a serious problem. Or you're seeking self-improvement in some areas. Perhaps you seek communion with your higher self, or your "Spirit Guide," or to pray to God. Then *direct* your meditation to your specific purpose. I believe regular meditation is more effective when it is focused on your particular objective.

On a purely practical level, the alpha state is considered by many to open the door to the subconscious mind, and there are numerous self-improvement programs based on using the alpha state for deprogramming the subconscious mind of negative responses and reprogramming it for positive ones. The theory is that the subconscious mind is nonjudgmental and purely reactive; and that if it reacts in ways that are detrimental to your well-being, it has been "programmed" wrongly and can be reprogrammed.

As a hypothetical example, a misguided parent may have often said, "You're so stupid! Can't you do anything right?" Unless you were strong enough as a child to totally reject the validity of that statement, you probably were programmed at the subconscious level with an inferiority complex that may still be subtly inhibiting you today. You *know* there's no truth to the accusation, and you try to put it behind you, but it still influences your self-image. In meditation, so the theory goes, you can "erase" that old recording by overriding it with a positive affirmation, firmly and repeatedly, while you're in the alpha state. This amounts to using the power of autosuggestion while your subconscious is in a suggestible state, and is considered by some to be a form of self-hypnosis. There are many variations on this theme of redirecting your proclivities through programming and reprogramming in alpha or self-hypnosis. There is no risk involved, and many persons use this or similar techniques with great benefit.

If you choose to reprogram, be sure to couch your new programming statements in *positive* terms (you say, "I am smart and capable"; don't say, "I am not stupid and incompetent"). And visualize yourself as *already having attained* that state and not as if you're going to achieve it at some future time. Compose your positive programming statement very carefully, and always use it exactly, word for word. When you reach the alpha state in the meditation countdown, address yourself mentally to your subconscious and repeat your positive affirmation many times. And don't expect miracles from a single meditation session; lifelong programming patterns commonly require many sessions to change. The process usually works for those who persist long enough.

If you'd prefer to address your higher self—your *Super*conscious—you can do that, too. But remember that your SC is a *thinking* level of mind, so don't insult it by trying to program it by rote repetition, but address your questions respectfully and be receptive to answers—which, if they come, may be very subtle, seeming to be nothing more than imagination. But where do you think your imagination comes from, anyhow? It's certainly not from your *sub*conscious!

And if your reach is even higher, it's but a step or two beyond your Superconscious to the spiritual realms. If you accept Spirit Guides, or God and an exalted hierarchy, then the meditative alpha state is a possible doorway to having your prayers heard, your questions answered, and your soul enlightened. This is so very much an area of personal belief that there are no singular rules that apply to everyone. You'll have to explore the alpha state for yourself to find out what works for you. For some, meditation has ultimately provided the way for literally "seeing the light" in ways that they can't express in words. Others try for years but never reach nirvana.

Among certain Far Eastern mystics, meditation is a way of life. Usually accompanied by years of purification and disciplining of the body, and by meditation for hours or days at a time, the search for ultimate enlightenment consumes their lives to the exclusion of nearly all earthly endeavors. This may be fine for the obsessed, but I don't believe that we are given this physical experience to spend that way; I think we are here to interact beneficially with our fellow humans, and that the essential value of meditation can be obtained with brief daily sessions to better equip us for our normal daily activities.

Commonplace among the doctrines of metaphysics is the concept of the seven "psychic energy" centers of the body, called the *chakras*, and the mysterious *kundalini* forces, which are said to be awakened by certain meditation practices, but these are beyond the scope of this introduction to meditation. There are any number of treatises on eastern mysticism that deal in depth with these concepts, should you care to pursue them.

Some schools of meditation teach that chanting, or that repeating a phrase called a *mantra*, is necessary to meditation. The essential function of this, in my opinion, is to provide a focus for your attention so that it won't wander about to the countless little thoughts that creep in when you're trying to clear your mind. And I will readily concede that the most difficult part of meditation is clearing your mind of irrelevant distractions. While I don't believe a *mantra* is essential, if you find that mentally repeating some focusing phrase helps you in meditation, then by all means use it. Like so many practices of metaphysics, the right way for you to meditate is the way that works *for you*. Use this introduction as a starting point, and grow further as you may choose to explore.

I will give here a step-by-step physical relaxation procedure and a mental countdown to the alpha state. You may want a friend to help lead you through it, although it's okay to semimemorize the steps and follow them in your mind. To be most effective, you should meditate twice a day, at the same times each day and not longer than fifteen to twenty minutes each time.

Before starting, you need to select a place where you're not likely to be interrupted. You may sit erect in a firm chair, feet flat on the floor and hands in your lap but not touching, or you may lie supine, on your back, on a bed or the floor, with your hands at your sides—that is, if you don't fall asleep during the exercise. (Not that there's any harm in falling asleep; you won't go into some deep trance that requires a kiss from a handsome prince or beautiful princess to break, but you can't focus on your goal if you fall asleep.) Or maybe you'd like my favorite for meditation: a recliner chair.

When you are in position, make a point of breathing deeply and slowly at least five times, as the initial step of bodily relaxation. Some teachers claim you should press against alternate sides of your nose, closing your nostrils so that you inhale through the right one and exhale through the left one—or is it vice versa? This is supposed to enhance your transition to an altered state of consciousness, and I'm sure it does—*if* you believe it does! Suit yourself about this.

I believe there is much merit in preparing for meditation—or any psychic experiment—by first visualizing yourself to be surrounded by a blanket or cocoon of pure white light. This represents a protective shield of positive energy that will repel any negative entity or influence that may be lurking about at any level of existence for an opening to your psyche. Always invoke this protective white light; visualize it around you, and *believe* it will protect you. After all, it can't do you any harm!

In the interest of clarity of instruction, I shortly will shift from narrative prose to declamatory statements typical of those used to lead the neophyte into deep relaxation and the meditative mental state. It can be helpful to have a friend as a partner to conduct you through the process the first few times by softly reading this countdown, with appropriate pauses, leaving your mind free to simply flow with the suggestions. Alternatively, you can familiarize yourself with the sequence of steps suggested here and mentally do your own countdown. This does divert part of your mind to the role of conductor and may require longer practice before you become proficient, but that's only a temporary drawback; either way, you'll soon find you can enter the relaxed state almost instantly whenever you want, needing neither external nor internal countdown. For now, though, be sure to have your partner allow what will seem like excessive pauses where they are indicated, or allow them in your mental countdown if you're doing this solo. Don't make the mistake of rushing things; slow and easy does it.

Now that you are in a comfortable position and secluded from distractions, close your eyes, and breathe deeply, rhythmically: one, . . . two, . . . three, . . . four, . . . five, . . . Listen for a moment to the sound of your breathing (pause), consciously set its depth and pace (pause), then leave it on "automatic" while you turn your full attention to my words (pause).

Next, I want you to imagine the sensation of relaxation beginning to envelop your feet. This sensation is caused by the release of all those subtle tensions, pressures, and discomforts in the muscles and tendons of your feet and ankles. You've become so accustomed to them that you hardly realized they were there, until you felt them leave!

As relaxation surrounds and enters your feet, it becomes almost tangible. You can actually *feel* it displacing all those sensations and leaving just a delightful sense of almost no feeling at all. And imagine, too, that—as your old tensions and aches are absorbed by this envelope of relaxation—all of your physical, emotional, and mental negativity also is being drawn out of your being.

This envelope of relaxation now slowly rises like a sleeve over your body, immersing your legs (long pause), your thighs (long pause), and now your hips. Your legs now seem to be almost weightless,

272

as though they were supported by water, and you find the sensation *very* enjoyable (pause).

And now the sleeve of relaxation is rising over your torso, and you can actually feel not only your muscles, but your internal organs, too, responding by relaxing and allowing your bodily processes to function effortlessly and healthfully (pause). And the relaxation reaches your chest, and you suddenly become aware that your breathing now is easier, deeper, and less labored.

While we're here at your lungs, take a moment for another visualization: imagine that each time you exhale, you are expelling all of the negative influences—physical, mental, and emotional—that you harbor within you; and that each time you inhale, you are drawing in positive influences—not only healthy air, but the glowing light of a universal creative energy that surrounds you everywhere. Perceive this energy to be both protective and productive for you, as it displaces the negative aspects you are expelling. Take another moment or two to reinforce this visualization: breathe out the negative (pause); breathe in the positive (pause).

The sleeve of relaxation has continued to slowly encompass you during all this, and it now has reached your shoulders and is branching down your arms and into your hands. You didn't realize you'd been slightly clenching your hands, did you, until you just now felt them *really* relax for the first time in—what's it been? Days? Weeks? Months? And now, right into your finger tips, where the relaxation is so intense that it almost tingles (pause).

And did you notice how this deep relaxation has

273

untied the knots of tension in your shoulders and neck? In your mind's eye, you can almost see some of those muscles unwinding, can't you, like rubber bands going limp. Even if you should never get beyond this point in your exploration of meditation, it'll still be worth it just for this deep relaxation. And the benefits will last long beyond the few minutes you spend getting here.

But it hasn't stopped yet! The blanket of relaxation now is moving over the back of your head and—did you know that even your scalp was tense? Feel it relax; feel the blood circulate more freely to the roots of your hair. And feel the lines of tension leave your forehead as the sleeve of relaxation begins to move down over your face. And your eyelids—you were keeping them tightly shut, but they'll stay closed without all that tension. Relax!

And your mouth and jaw—other body parts that stay under a lot of tension. You can *really* feel the relaxation enter them! Your lips and teeth may part just a bit, and your head may tilt forward slightly but not all the way down to your chest; there is an upright head position that allows the greatest relaxation of the supporting muscles and the throat (pause).

You are now completely relaxed; more completely, probably, than you have been in a long time. Before we proceed, take a few moments to savor the sheer physical delight of being so relaxed that your conscious mind is scarcely aware of your body. Visualize again the process of breathing out the negative and breathing in the positive, feeling yourself seem to become more "open," more uncluttered, more buoyant with each breath you take. You may feel like drifting off to sleep, but you will not; you will continue to flow with my words as you move into experiences far more fascinating than sleep. (Pause for thirty seconds.)

At this point, we have relaxed the body enough that it demands no attention—no awareness—from your conscious mind; the next order of business is to relax the mind and free it of the clutter of niggling thoughts, concerns, and worries that compete for attention during our waking hours. Since we want to use the mind creatively, on a level of effective personal reality, it is desirable to narrow down its focus to a specific area that leaves no room for stray thoughts. There are any number of ways to do this, one of which will work best for you. As you become more accustomed to venturing inward, you should experiment with different techniques to find the best one for you. And if you have reached this stage through your own preferred relaxation technique, I suggest you pick up our exercise at this point.

Returning now to the declamatory voice, I will suggest a focusing technique.

Now that you are physically relaxed, I want you to ignore your body and look around your mind. What do you see—or hear? (Pause.) There is a continual "muttering" of inconsequential thoughts rolling about the periphery of your awareness, isn't there? Perhaps along with the scrap of a song that keeps intruding over and over, or the sour taste of someone's biting, thoughtless remark, made so long ago that everyone else has forgotten it. This is useless clutter now; just sweep it into a pile and shut it behind one of the doors in your mind. Be sure it's tightly locked; wisps of that clutter will try to reenter your awareness, so when you sense pressure from some banished thought, push it back into the dim recesses of your awareness. Now—*inside your head*—turn your mind's eye to your mental-image screen; the same screen you use for sleep dreams, daydreams, and imagination. If it's not blank, wipe it clear and concentrate on the center of it (pause).

Look steadily and intently. Ignore everything but my words; you will not be distracted by outside sounds, bodily sensations, or stray thoughts. Concentrate on your mental screen (pause). Now, in the very center of that screen, you see a tiny pinpoint of intense light. It may be white, or blue, or whatever you personally prefer, but it is bright, and it seems to be slowly growing larger!

While you're staring at this expanding point of light, imagine that it's an image that the movie camera of your mind can zoom into and enlarge to fill the screen. In fact, what you are seeing is a very distant view of your own private Shangri-la that you created several chapters back; your idyllic retreat from the pressures and cares of the external world. When it zooms in close enough for you to see details, you will find it to be exactly as you last visualized it. But before we zoom in, I need

276

just a moment to put your creative powers into perspective.

It is essential for you to understand that there are no rules or restrictions on what you seek, visualize, and create. In this private realm *you* are god and you can create exactly what you want! If you didn't create your secret retreat before, do it now! And if you already have, take a few moments now to enter, secure the premises, and relax into your surroundings in preparation for seeking the object of your meditation. (Pause for one minute.)

Now you are ready to focus on your meditation objective. Since you have made your personal choice among the possibilities of self-programming, communing with your Superconscious, seeking attunement with God, or whatever, I can help only by remaining silent for several minutes while you proceed. (Pause for three minutes.)

(Softly): Now it's time to conclude your focus and prepare to return to the external world. You rise and, looking to see that you've left all as you want it, you leave your hideaway and secure it against intruders.

And now you walk slowly away, and when you look back, you find you have stepped outside of your mental screen and that your Shangri-la is receding into the distance as your mental lens zooms back from the scene. And you're becoming more aware of sounds that you weren't noticing before, and you're becoming aware of your bodily sensations again.

As you approach full awareness, you will find that you feel as rested, relaxed, and comfortable as you do after a good night's sleep. This is one real, tangible benefit of meditating in your inner sanctum, even if you never obtain any others.

And now, on my count of three, you will slowly open your eyes and be fully attuned to the world of external reality:

one (pause);
two (pause);
and *three*. You are now awake and feeling great.

Any time you detach yourself from external reality for a few minutes, you can visit your Shangri-la for respite from the pressures of the world. With practice, you may find you can relax and enter your inner world even when the surroundings are not ideal. So long as you are not subject to interruption by someone addressing you directly, you may be able to meditate in, say, a moving bus or train, or seated in the theater, or at home in front of the television set that someone else is watching. The more you practice, the sooner you will learn what surroundings you require for success, and the sooner you will develop a unique and consistent technique that works fastest and most effectively for you.

I caution you against one possible misuse of your personal retreat: withdrawal. Shangri-la is a *temporary* haven for marshalling your resources, meditating, and refining your strategies for coping with external reality. It is *not* an alternate reality intended to shelter you from the responsibility of interacting with the real world and should not be resorted to as such, although it may serve for short-term recovery from an uncommonly traumatic occurrence. Those who retreat permanently or principally into their own inner realities are failing their roles in our physical world, and are rightly judged by society to be deranged. Don't let the peace and perfection of your inner sanctum lure you into this mistake. Use relaxation and meditation constructively and your world will be the better for it.

Afterword

OUR GANG

I have bought golden opinions from all sorts of people.

—Shakespeare
Macbeth

Well, did you succeed in communicating with your Superconscious? I hope so. But if you didn't, don't give up yet. Keep trying every day and you'll surely break through eventually. Or your SC will break through your conscious-mind barriers, if that's where the difficulty lies.

One reason I hope you succeeded is purely selfish: if all this is new to you, confirmation of the mere existence of your own Superconscious is a major step toward your acceptance of some of the metaphysical and spiritual concepts I've set forth, and that's a step toward the objective of this book.

More to the point, if you can establish effective

communication with your higher self, you have your own personal authority against whom to bounce any of those concepts set forth here that you may doubt. As I've said from the very beginning, the only person with the right to decide what you will believe is you. Now you will understand that I mean this in the sense of the *total* you, by which I include your higher self.

This book contains information gleaned from "higher" sources both incarnate and discarnate. Several years of research with individuals and the Metaphysical Research Group[1] have led me to incorporate these concepts into my own working belief structure.

Before I introduce you to "Our Gang" of sources, I'll tell you something about myself:

A product of midwestern Protestant rearing, I have always believed in the "conventional" concept of a human spiritual essence that transcends physical existence. A formal education in the physical sciences failed to dispel that belief, but it did give me a strong appreciation for making logical deductions from empirical evidence, and for suspending judgment until that evidence becomes compelling. It also gave me insight into the rigid structures of evidence upon which orthodox scientists build their realities and the resulting limitations imposed on those scientists' abilities to openly contemplate evidence of alternate realities. I therefore comprehend, even though I may sometimes

---

[1]The metaphysical study group that evolved from the Richmond, Virginia chapter of the Jupiter Movement founded by Bruce Born.

deplore, their customary inability to concede the slightest credibility to the body of subjective evidence that exists in the literature in such considerable quantities.

This insight has served me well during my ensuing occupational years in various aspects of communications. It also has kept my mind open and my interest active in the many fascinating areas of the paranormal, regardless of its disparagement by most scientists. Until a few years, ago, however, my interest was principally passive and solitary; I read widely in the field, but had no personal acquaintances who either actively pursued similar interests or experienced paranormal events in their own lives.

Upon the advent of more leisure time as my children approached adulthood, I gravitated toward various small groups actively studying metaphysics and psychic phenomena. It was in one of these, the Jupiter Movement, that the existence of the "hidden," *intellectual* mind-aspect of the Spirit—the Superconscious—was demonstrated through various manifestations. Even though I have always accepted the existence of a personal Spirit, and I had read Edgar Cayce's allusions to a superconscious level of awareness, it took my participation in group research to put it together within my own working reality structure. After all, to finally appreciate that a portion of your own being is thinking independently and interacting with its counterparts in realms outside of your normal conscious awareness is both fascinating and awesome. And humbling: suddenly the rational, conscious

282

mortal around which you've built your entire self-image is reduced to only an aspect of some larger, mysterious entity that is the *real* you. Just when you think you finally know yourself, that you finally "have it all together," this enigmatic additional facet is revealed. There seems to be no end to the quest for knowledge of self! Isn't that why you're reading this?

So much for myself; on to others of "Our Gang". The Jupiter Movement philosophy was strongly grounded in the metaphysical revelations of Edgar Cayce, probably the most thoroughly documented psychic of this century. Although he never wrote a book, all of his trance readings were recorded by a secretary, and many others have written extensively about him. If you are interested in more detail than is given here, I refer you to books such as Thomas Sugrue's *There Is a River* and Jess Stearn's *The Sleeping Prophet*.

Edgar Cayce was born in 1877 in Christian County, Kentucky. As a boy, he was quiet, reserved, and apparently a slow learner. The earliest manifestation of unusual abilities was his discovery that he could absorb, verbatim, the contents of an entire book simply by sleeping with it under his pillow. This ability carried him successfully through the nine years of rural schooling that constituted his formal education.

Cayce developed a keen interest in the Bible at the age of ten, when most of his contemporaries were occupied with sports and other typical boyhood activities. He determined to read it completely through once a year; why he didn't elect simply to sleep on it isn't clear, but reading it through yearly became a lifelong practice.

His interest in the Bible paralleled his youthful desire to become a preacher. He built a lean-to retreat in an isolated spot, to which he retired daily for his Bible studies. In the spring of his thirteenth year, he received at his retreat a "visitation" by what he perceived to be an angel, who addressed him in a feminine voice. When she asked young Cayce the one thing he most wanted, it was for the ability to help others, especially sick children. Little could he have guessed then that he would later display that ability in a most remarkable manner.

His first manifestation of record indeed did help a sick child: himself. Suffering a seemingly innocuous spinal blow from a baseball, the teen-aged Edgar began acting very strangely. During a period of troubled and apparently delirious sleep, he instructed his mother to prepare a poultice and apply it to him overnight. The ingredients he specified seemed harmless enough, so she complied, whereupon the boy awoke in the morning completely normal and with no conscious memory of the interval following the accident.

From this episode, Cayce learned that he could somehow tap sources of knowledge while he was asleep that were far beyond his education and conscious experience. Awake, he seemed a rather simple, plain, highly religious individual; asleep or in trance, he confidently displayed a vast knowledge of medical and metaphysical subjects. It was clear that he possessed a highly unusual access to *some-*

thing beyond his conscious mind, and he found that this source of knowledge could be as beneficial to others as it had proved to him.

So the pattern was set. From early adulthood, Edgar Cayce responded to requests for help by going into trance and delivering readings containing information helpful to the requester. The great bulk of his readings, especially in his earlier years, were in response to questions of physical health. The remedies suggested by his trance personality often were unorthodox but usually effective, and it was not even necessary for the afflicted person to be present. All Cayce needed was a name, and his higher source(s) would zero in on the individual, wherever he might be, diagnose the problem, and suggest a remedy. Thanks to the fact that every trance reading was recorded by a secretary, subsequent researchers have been able to follow up on the thousands of readings and have found them to have a remarkably high percentage of accuracy.

Edgar Cayce was not to realize his ambition to become a minister. Considering his gift to be God-given, he did not charge for trance readings, but supported his family variously as a book-store employee and as a photographer. He did manage, though, to teach Sunday School in his local Christian Church for most of his life.

Meanwhile, his fame as trance reader grew. Not all was smooth; he suffered many indignities at the hands of nonbelievers determined to unmask what they considered to be unmitigated fraud and the unqualified practice of medicine. Then, in 1944, the first edition of *There Is a River* popularized Cayce's talents and he was overwhelmed by requests for readings. Feeling an obligation to help all seekers, he began to spend more and more time in trance, while also maintaining his occupation. He collapsed from the strain in August 1944, and died of stroke the following September, ending a most remarkable life.

But his works have not died. There are transcripts of thirty thousand trance readings on file with his surviving Association for Research and Enlightenment (A.R.E.) in Virginia Beach, Virginia. Members of A.R.E. still are indexing and cross-referencing this mountain of information, and are disseminating the results to thousands of other members and interested people around the world. And virtually every city in the United States has Cayce Study Groups, whose members discuss and endeavor to apply the philosophies that follow from Cayce's revelations.

It's true that Edgar Cayce began his trance activities as a medical advisor, but it was inevitable that among thirty thousand trances there would be responses to many nonmedical questions. Piecing together isolated but subject-related statements made in different readings, a metaphysical structure of spiritual reality emerges. There is a remarkable consistency in statements made as much as thirty years apart, many of them troublesome to Cayce because they seemed to contradict some of the conventional Protestant church doctrine in which he was so thoroughly steeped. Like many trance readers, he was unaware of the information he gave while in trance, and he often was incredulous upon hearing his words read back.[2]

When asked in trance who or what this source was, Cayce never identified it as an aspect of himself. When the question subsequently was addressed by researchers in the Jupiter Movement, it was given that his source was indeed his Superconscious, addressable by the name of Karpin, who spoke as the editorial "we" of Cayce's trances.

It was natural for this question to arise within the Jupiter Movement, which had its roots in the metaphysical revelations contained in Cayce's readings and undertook to research and develop them further. The movement's founder, Bruce Born, characterized it as "an organization that teaches the realities of metaphysics, which in turn tells us the truth about our reasons for being here."

Since the Jupiter Movement was instrumental in the embryonic stages of formulating the metaphysical concepts addressed in this book, it is interesting to review its beginnings—if only to illustrate how a very conventional individual can find his life completely changed through higher-level influences.

Bruce Born was reared a devout Roman Catholic and lived a very ordinary life for his first forty-odd years. As he tells it:

---

[2]While it will not convince an observing skeptic, the total *unawareness*—literal unconsciousness—the trance reader may experience while his or her physical body is speaking coherently and at length is satisfactory proof to that reader that something other than his/her normal consciousness is manifesting.

I had no idea what "psychic" or "metaphysics" meant, and I had no desire to learn what they meant. My gradual awakening started with reading the book *There Is a River*, by Tom Sugrue. This is a biography of Edgar Cayce, the greatest psychic the world has ever known. After studying this and other Cayce material until I knew them quite thoroughly, I then conducted thirteen seminars in south Jersey, southeastern Pennsylvania, and Wilmington, Delaware, called "An Introduction to the Edgar Cayce Philosophy," subtitled "A Crash Course in Metaphysics." Then, following a visit to the A.R.E., in Virginia Beach, which is the headquarters of the Edgar Cayce Foundation, and having meetings there with several of the staff people, I organized a local chapter of the Cayce "Search for God" Home Study Group.

The single most important revelation that came out of this study group was the fact that within each of our physical bodies there resides an immortal Spirit. Later I learned that this spirit has a conscious and a superconscious mind, as well as memory, emotions, and personality. . . . A short time after that came the most dramatic event in the unfolding of my psychic development: the discovery that I was one of those extremely rare, gifted people who can have direct communication with the superconscious mind of their Spirit. Slowly, gradually, this communication improved to the point where I discovered that we could actually carry on a conversation. He told me that his name was Astar, and then he started dictating psychic readings to me that became the text material for these [Jupiter Movement] classes.

There are many different types of psychic readers, and I am what is known as a psychic *scribe*, which means that all of my readings are written. . . . It's like a secretary, who puts on a Dictaphone headset to type a letter which her boss has dictated. She has no idea of what he's going to say; she just types whatever she hears. Although our communication is non-verbal, I do exactly the same thing. I just write, word for word, what is dictated to me.

Thus was the Jupiter Movement born. Not only did Bruce obtain Astar's confirmation of many of Cayce's revelations, along with numerous additional details regarding the nature and abilities of the superconscious mind; he also was given the mission to teach those who would listen. So strong is the sense of mission imparted by Astar that Bruce relinquished his occupation to teach full time. He and his wife, Jeann, periodically change their residence from city to city, at Astar's direction, to establish classes. It was one of these that provided my indoctrination into the realities of the Superconscious.

Astar is a principal purveyor of knowledge of the Superconscious. He has dictated nearly fifty papers that have been used in Bruce's classes, treating metaphysical subjects as diverse as hypnosis and earth's prehistory. To the extent that my personal concepts are shaped by my exposure to those papers, Astar must be considered one of the authorities behind this book. I have not, however, automatically and uncritically accepted every pronouncement of his; I've applied the same independence of judgment that I urge you to exercise in evaluating the precepts of this book. Nothing goes into my belief structure that fails my own judgment of its validity and compatibility with my existing structure, and much of that which does pass the test of acceptability is incorporated on a tentative basis, to allow for revision in the light of future enlargement of knowledge. Therefore it would be erroneous to hold Astar responsible for statements made here, excepting those specifically attributed to him.[3]

Since my exposure to Astar, I have encountered a number of other Superconscious intellects who manifest forcefully through their own mortals, if incarnate, or through various mediumistic mechanisms if discarnate. Among the more credible ones is Mary, the Superconscious of an individual who was extremely familiar to me. Mary seems every bit as forthright and committed to truth as was her mortal, and I hold her pronouncements in high regard.

---

[3] It is understandable that one who receives dictated messages having explicit content purporting to be absolute truths would not condone conflicting concepts proposed by students in his classes. Yet a number of us in the Richmond chapter of JM insisted on the freedom to embrace alternatives we found more palatable to our various belief structures. The ultimate result of this was separation from the parent organization and formation of a very loosely chartered one called the Metaphysical Research Group.

Just as Astar avowedly has a mission to teach, Mary states that her mission—in part—is to assist with this book. It was she, in fact, who confirmed my growing conviction that one of *my* missions is to write it. So Mary is another superconscious "authority" behind the information and concepts presented here.

Apart from my close association with her mortal counterpart, I attribute high credibility to Mary's informational statements because of her vantage point in the nonmaterial realms: she presently is discarnate. Unlike Astar, she doesn't psychically dictate her pronouncements for the perceiving mortal to transcribe; she utilizes what may be a modern form of automatic writing by manipulating Marianne's hands on a typewriter keyboard.

(Marianne is the multitalented psychic to whom I am married, and I accept her assertion that, even though she is fully conscious during the process, it is not *her* mind that is volitionally directing her hands while Mary is communicating with us via typewriter.)

As I did in the case of Astar, I must enter a disclaimer here regarding Mary. Even though her input figures prominently in the content of this book, it would not be accurate to attribute any general statements to her, excepting in those instances where I explicitly do so.

Most of the concepts presented here have survived confirmation by several presumably knowledgeable sources. For students of many subjects, library research is acceptable, but interviews with authorities in their respective fields are preferable.

For the subject of metaphysics, however, library references are mostly as speculative as this book is, so I consider those intellects presently active—at whatever levels—in metaphysical pursuits to be more authoritative. Among these are associates in our local research group and their Superconsciouses. Notable among the latter are Nathan, who is Marianne's Superconscious, and Mia, who is Sandie's. We've also had some information imparted by Sam, once related to Mary, although we are in contact with him only rarely since his reincarnation a couple of years ago. His replacement, a discarnate known as Cecil, shares much of Sam's light-hearted philosophy.

It would be convenient if all these higher intellects always agreed on every metaphysical question posed to them, but they don't! Mary may disagree on a point with Astar (and often does); Nathan may disagree with both. It is important to bear in mind that superconscious minds, like conscious ones, have individual personalities, individual opinions and biases, individual perceptions—in short, unique personal realities. Complete agreement right down to minutiae is no more probable among them than it is among conscious minds at the mortal level. Since we usually cannot define absolutes with any degree of confidence, we seek an understanding that seems workable within the framework of subjective practical reality. In the process, we sometimes reach a conclusion that directly opposes a position stated by one of our sources.

To further complicate the question of certainty, we are burdened by the rule that no Superconscious is permitted to provide an accuracy of one hundred percent (Mary and Astar agree on this); that we are not to be handed anything on a silver platter, so to speak. How, then, do I arrive at some of the conclusions presented here? In part, through conscious intellectual evaluation, as is expected of each of us. Beyond this, Richard, my Superconscious, is my bottom-line authority, just as your Superconscious must be yours. Richard's input usually is extremely subtle and not readily distinguishable from my conscious deliberations, thanks to his insistence that I first think things through on the conscious level. But in important matters, my conscious conclusions often will be supplemented or countered by an impression—an intuitive conviction—that my position "feels right" or "feels wrong." I have come to realize that this is how Richard works, and he rarely misleads me. So, to the extent that he influences my conclusions and statements, Richard is another authority behind this book.

So there you have "Our Gang," the assorted personalities behind this effort to enlarge your perception of reality and the purpose of existence. None of these is infallible, but all are knowledgeable and highly motivated, and each is hopeful that *your* Superconscious will lead you to genuinely benefit from these pages. The rest is up to you.

About the Author

ROBERT H. CODDINGTON is a charter member and past chairman of the Richmond Metaphysical Research Group, and a charter member of the Virginia Association for the Non-physical Sciences. He is the author of *Modern Radio Broadcasting* and numerous articles in trade magazines such as *Broadcast Engineering*, *CEE*, *db*, and *CUFOS Associate Newsletter*. He has done extensive writing for broadcast and audiovisual productions. He lives with his wife in Richmond, Virginia.